Total Purchasing
a model for locality commissioning

Edited by

Rod Smith
Fran Butler
Mike Powell

with a Foreword by

Chris Ham

D1331778

Radcliffe Medical Press
Oxford and New York

© 1996 Rod Smith, Fran Butler and Mike Powell

Radcliffe Medical Press Ltd
18 Marcham Road, Abingdon, Oxon OX14 1AA, UK

Radcliffe Medical Press, Inc.
141 Fifth Avenue, New York, NY 10010, USA

British Library Cataloguing in Publication Data

A catalogue record for this book is available from the British Library.

ISBN 1 85775 146 9

Library of Congress Cataloging-in-Publication Data.

Total purchasing : a model for locality commissioning / edited by Rod Smith, Fran Butler,
and Mike Powell ; with a foreword by Chris Ham.
    p.   cm.
  Includes bibliographical references and index.
  ISBN 1–85775–146–9
  1. Fundholding (Medical economics)—Great Britain.   I. Smith, Rod, Dr.
II. Butler, Fran.   III. Powell, Mike.
  RA410.55.G7T68   1996
  362.1′068′1—dc20   96–11413
                                                                    CIP

Typeset by Advance Typesetting Ltd, Oxon
Printed and bound in Great Britain by Biddles Ltd, Guildford and King's Lynn

Contents

List of contributors

Dr Gary Bolger   Consultant in Public Health Medicine, Berkshire Health Authority, Pendragon House, 59 Bath Road, Reading RG30 2BA

Fran Butler   Project Manager, BIPP, c/o Berkshire Health Authority, Pendragon House, 59 Bath Road, Reading RG30 2BA

Janet Fitzgerald   Fund Manager, Balmore Park Surgery, 59a Hemdean Road, Caversham, Reading RG4 7SS

Dr Stephen Henry   General Practitioner, Lovemead Group Practice, Roundstone Surgery, Polebarn Circus, Trowbridge, Wiltshire BA14 7EG

Alan Hudson   Head of Costing and Pricing, Royal Berkshire and Battle Hospitals NHS Trust, Royal Berkshire Hospital, London Road, Reading RG1 5AN

Richard Mills   Head of Strategy, Berkshire Health Authority, Pendragon House, 59 Bath Road, Reading RG30 2BA

Alastair Mitchell-Baker   Director of Strategy and Service Development, Royal Berkshire and Battle Hospitals NHS Trust, Royal Berkshire Hospital, London Road, Reading RG1 5AN

Lesley Morris   General Manager, Lovemead Group Practice, Roundstone Surgery, Polebarn Circus, Trowbridge, Wiltshire BA14 7EG

Dr Mike Powell   General Practitioner, The Boathouse Surgery, Whitchurch Road, Pangbourne RG8 7DP

Dr Jonathan Shapiro   Senior Fellow, Health Services Management Centre, School of Public Policy, Park House, 40 Edgbaston Road, Birmingham B15 2RT

Sharon-Esther Sloan   Corporate Business Manager, West Berkshire Priority Care Services NHS Trust, Pendragon House, 59 Bath Road, Reading RG30 2BA

Dr Rod Smith   General Practitioner, Balmore Park Surgery, 59a Hemdean Road, Caversham, Reading RG4 7SS

Nicola Walsh   Honorary Fellow, Health Services Management Centre, School of Public Policy, Park House, 40 Edgbaston Road, Birmingham B15 2RT

Foreword

GP fundholding has been one of the great surprises of the NHS reforms. From small beginnings, it has come to cover over half the population in England, and its popularity has led the government to introduce the option of both total purchasing and community fundholding in 1996.

The importance of fundholding is that it has shifted the balance of power within the NHS. GPs are able to exert greater influence over service delivery and to bring about benefits for patients. This has proved uncomfortable for those providing hospital and community health services whose traditional methods of working have been challenged by fundholders. Total purchasing extends the influence of GPs and holds out the promise of changes in those services encompassed within fundholding for the first time.

For GPs about to embark on the total purchasing route, this book offers a fascinating insight into what is happening at the frontiers of the NHS reforms. And for health authorities and the NHS Trusts, it indicates the challenge that lies ahead.

Total Purchasing: a model for locality commissioning imparts a key message: total purchasing is breaking down the isolation of GPs and is encouraging collaboration between practices. As a consequence, a new kind of primary care organization is emerging. Where this will lead in the longer term is unclear, but already the outlines of an alternative future can be detected. This is as much to do with primary care provision as with commissioning.

Innovations in service provision made by the Berkshire Integrated Purchasing Unit are described in the book. Although the project is still in its infancy, the GPs involved are beginning to explore new ways of doing things and have started to question established practices. The book also demonstrates that total purchasing is hard work. Taking on responsibility for the whole budget is both complex and time consuming and calls for an investment in management on a scale not seen before. The unanswered question is whether the transaction costs of total purchasing will be outweighed by the benefits. It is this question, among others, that is being addressed by the evaluation team. This book suggests that a promising beginning has been made, although a great deal remains to be done.

At a time when the government has launched a great debate about the future of primary care, *Total Purchasing* offers some important pointers. It must be read with interest by all those involved in the NHS.

Professor Chris Ham
Director
Health Services Management Unit
University of Birmingham

March 1996

An introduction to total purchasing
Rod Smith

Fundholding has proved remarkably successful, despite the political con-
troversy surrounding its introduction. By 1995/6 41% of the population
was covered by fundholding, compared with only 7% coverage in 1991/2,
the first year of fundholding. Fundholding initially covered only a limited
range of hospital and community services, mainly elective services, although
the services covered have gradually increased since its introduction, with
a major extension to include many extra community services from 1 April
1993, including community nursing, chiropody, dietetics, community
and mental health services and services for people with learning disabilities. Nevertheless fundholders only control about 20% of their patients'
resources.

Many fundholders and indeed NHS Trusts felt that the list of goods and
services purchased by fundholders was illogical, and there was much
confusion on the ground about the fine detail of what was in and out – for
example, infertility outpatient services were outside fundholding and
gynaecology outpatients were within it – so it was often difficult for fundholders and Trusts to know whether the fundholder or his health authority
should pay for such a service.

The fact that emergency admissions continued to be purchased by health
authorities while most outpatient care and elective surgery was purchased
by fundholders led to fundholders not necessarily becoming involved in
strategic purchasing. For example in the short term it might be advantageous for a fundholder to purchase elective orthopaedic surgery from
a distant provider or a private hospital, which might in the longer term
damage local emergency trauma services. Purchasing all services will bring
fundholders fully into the strategic arena.

Of course there were good reasons for initially only giving fundholders
a limited remit as risks for practices with relatively small lists were felt
to be too high. A single car crash might seriously embarrass a small
purchaser, so A&E was initially left with the district health authority
(DHA). The confusion about what was in and out of fundholding also

made fundholding difficult to evaluate, as critics were able to say that fundholders were overfunded and evidence to refute or confirm this was impossible to produce. Critics also believed that fundholders artificially made elective fundholding procedures emergencies to avoid paying for them.

Despite all the problems fundholding has been remarkably successful, with falling waiting lists and improved community services in fundholding practices and fundholders saving about 3.5% of their budgets in 1992/3.

This success led the government to announce four pilot sites for total purchasing by GPs in 1994/5 (in Bromsgrove, Berkshire, Runcorn and Worth Valley). Three of these sites involved groups of practices to increase the population base and decrease the risk of volatile activity inherent in purchasing for a small population, although the fourth was a single practice. In October 1994 the Secretary of State announced a further major expansion of fundholding, with extensions to the standard scheme, a simple entry community fundholding and a major expansion of total purchasing to establish a further 25 pilot sites. The NHS Executive was overwhelmed with applications and eventually established over 50 pilot sites involving about two and a quarter million patients. Many potential pilot sites were disappointed, and some have formed unofficial pilots with their health authorities, while others are waiting for the second wave of total purchasing, which will involve a further 20 sites in 1996/7. All of the pilot sites are to be evaluated by the NHS Executive.

Total purchasing in action

Unlike fundholding there is little central guidance on the development of total purchasing and there has been no primary legislation to allow it to happen, so fundholders have to develop local agreements with their local health authority, whose budget for services outside fundholding they will need to share.

Implications for GPs

Most total purchasing groups involve groups of GPs in different practices, who may have quite different ways of working and of using resources. As they come to share a budget and develop a strategy, they will need to work closely together. Conventional fundholding will need to continue alongside the total fund, usually with the individual historically-set practice fundholding budgets top-sliced from the group's total fund and run individually by each practice. Agreement will have to be reached between the participating practices on how over- and underspends on the shared extension to the fundholding component of the fund are to be dealt with; for example if the number of emergencies are increasing in only one practice, how are the budgetary overspends to be dealt with? Will all the fundholders have to rescue the budget overspend from their conventional fundholding budgets or will the health authority bail out the overspender?

Implications for health authorities

The health authority will need to set up monitoring systems to ensure that the total purchasing group is working to its budget and delivering agreed national and local targets. There will also need to be local arrangements to align the total purchasing group's strategy with the rest of the DHA's – for example on local mental health provision, where a local large hospital is to be closed, or on cancer services. Public health input for the fundholding group will also be important. Agreement needs to be reached on a budget setting mechanism. One of the great attractions of total purchasing is that a capitation model of funding can be developed, something which has proved impossible to develop in conventional fundholding because of the complexities of what is in and out of fundholding.

Implications for acute and community Trusts

Trusts will need to make major adjustments for total purchasers. Many acute Trusts still have contracts that price emergencies on average specialty cost, which fundholders are unlikely to accept. One of the attractions of total purchasing is that if GPs can reduce lengths of stay in hospital, they can bring resources out of the hospital to support patients in the community. GPs have had many years of talk of work and resources coming into the community but have noted more success in the transfer of work than in the transfer of resources.

Why this book?

This book is written for all those working in Trusts, health authorities, social services and general practices who have to enact total purchasing; it is designed to help them speed up the processes that we had to develop from first principles. It is edited by two GPs and the project manager from the Berkshire Integrated Purchasing Project – a total purchasing pilot involving six practices and 85 000 patients – and has contributors from acute and community Trusts and from the health authority. In addition to the Berkshire pilot site the book also includes a study of the Wiltshire and Bath pilot, to give a wider perspective. Inevitably in such a fast-moving field there will be areas that we have not covered in great detail. This book gives the reader a general introduction to the scale of the task of total purchasing.

As well as being useful to total purchasers we hope that the book will be useful to those developing locality purchasing outside fundholding. Locality purchasing, like total purchasing, is concerned with the development of primary care-led purchasing by involving GPs in the local development of health services and giving them incentives to change their own behaviour and the behaviour of other health care workers who look after their patients, to improve the health service. To be successful locality purchasing will need to take on some of the lessons of fundholding – ownership of decision making by GPs, recognition by all GPs that a resource wasted on one patient is a lost opportunity for another and, perhaps most importantly of all, devolution of resources to the locality acting as a strong encouragement to change. The origins of the belief among fundholders that 'one GP with a cheque-book is worth ten on a committee' are uncertain, but it hides a simple truth that Trusts listen more attentively and act more rapidly when there are financial consequences to inaction. We believe that total purchasing provides a model for locality purchasing and that over time there will be little difference between successful total purchasing and locality purchasing, regardless of whether its origins lie in fundholding or non-fundholding.

2

Total purchasing – the health authority perspective

Gary Bolger and Richard Mills

This chapter gives an overview of a total purchasing project from the health authority's perspective. It is aimed at GPs and health authorities who are considering such a venture and builds on 18 months' experience of the authority in Berkshire.

The chapter gives the background to total purchasing expectations that the authority had (and continues to have), the systems that were needed, public health involvement, calculation of budgets (including the advantages and disadvantages of different types), accountability and lessons learned.

Background

Once the initial changes following the introduction of the NHS reforms had settled down and purchasers had become established, most health authorities started to consider the development of more locally-based purchasing. This took many different forms but is generally known as locality purchasing. At the same time a number of the small health authorities were merging into larger county groupings, and they were keen not to lose a local focus.

In parallel but separate from this, regional health authorities (RHAs) and family health services authorities (FHSAs) had been developing fundholding, which in some areas (including Berkshire) had by the third wave (in 1993) come to encompass a significant proportion of the population. Furthermore, some of these fundholders had come together to form local groupings to pool resources and expertise, one of these being the West Berkshire Fundholding Consortium.

Expectations of total purchasing

Therefore in their different ways, both the health authorities and some fundholders were keen to achieve a focus on purchasing for a particular area. The health authority's expectations of total purchasing were as follows. It would:

- build on strengths of fundholding
- build on the strengths of the health authority
- encourage GPs to be involved in wider purchasing
- lead to innovative service changes
- recognize the role of GPs as a key influential group
- be recognized as part of developments in the NHS
- improve clinical effectiveness in primary and secondary care.

Fundholders were perceived by the health authority to have particular expertise in purchasing services for individual patients, as they make the individual referrals themselves. They had proved effective in achieving service changes and quality improvements with providers. The health authority felt that its strengths were in strategic analysis, population-based planning, technology assessment, knowledge of wider NHS environment and national policy, secondary care service changes, risk management and managing larger contracts and those for tertiary referrals, including those with providers in Oxford and London. There was therefore a view that bringing the two methods of purchasing together was both logical and advantageous for both parties.

Having taken the decision to support the project, the health authority had to consider what role it should play and how. There was much discussion and negotiation within the project board over this, and the health authority input was mainly in the following areas:

- allowing the project considerable autonomy
- providing strategic context and input
- assisting in the selection of the project manager and providing her with ongoing support
- identifying the roles of individuals in the authority in relation to the project

- organizing support staff to undertake contract management
- providing accommodation for the project manager and team (and their employment)
- calculating budgets.

Setting up systems

Early selection of an effective project manager with the right range of skills was a key factor. There was much work to be done and few precedents on how to do it. The individual needed to be able to negotiate effectively and to have information skills to establish the necessary infrastructure and systems. These systems are dealt with in more detail in Chapter 7. From the health authority's perspective, it was important that the new systems were robust and effective to ensure that the Berkshire Integrated Purchasing Project (BIPP) could manage its own budget.

The authority appointed a purchasing manager and an information manager to form a BIPP central office. They ensured that:

- the project manager was supported in negotiation
- the contracts would be effectively monitored
- the information analysis of both current and future activities could be undertaken for both contract monitoring and needs assessment.

Ten per cent of BIPP activity is with 'external providers', and these are managed by the authority on behalf of BIPP. This both saves BIPP some extracontractual referral (ECR) costs and maximizes benefits from the authority's specialist contract monitoring expertise.

The project required considerable staff input from the authority, both at director and senior manager level, to ensure that the authority's interests were observed and also that the project could integrate effectively with the authority's systems as well as those of fundholding and the FHSA.

Public health and total purchasing

Public health is a medical specialty whose role is to look after the health of the population rather than individuals. The position has some similarity to that of GPs who consider themselves to be responsible for the health of everyone on their list and sometimes have to balance the competing needs of individual patients for their time. However, public health physicians tend to see this role as looking after much larger populations (perhaps hundreds of thousands) and rarely get involved in the management of individual patients. The exception to this is that part of the specialty is devoted to communicable disease control, when individual patient management is much more to the fore, and more recently ECR authorization.

Public health physicians, in order to take on this role, receive training in epidemiology, statistics, health economics, sociology, management and health promotion (as well as communicable disease). These skills are useful in monitoring the health of populations, needs assessment, data analysis, planning services and evaluating interventions and ways of delivering services. These skills should also be useful to total purchasing GPs, who should seek to obtain significant public health input into their project.

In addition to the skills that public health physicians have, most will also bring considerable experience of local services, Trusts further afield, successes and failures at changing services, the organization of Trusts and health authorities, and local and national policies. Total purchasing schemes should make good use of these skills and experience for help and advice over proposed changes in services, evaluation of new and existing services, and existing national and local policies. Perhaps, however, the most immediate use total purchasing pilots will have for public health physicians is for advice over ECR management.

Budgets for total purchasing

The development of a fair budget for a total purchasing project is a crucial step. Unfortunately it is also one of the most difficult to decide upon with a large degree of confidence. The goal should be to develop a budget regarded as fair by those participating in total purchasing, and also one of which others, particularly surrounding practices or populations, would not be envious.

Ideally a health authority, in establishing such a budget, should involve as many interested parties as it can. The discussions should include the health authority and the practices involved and also representatives of other practices and the large Trusts serving the fundholding population. The reason for this is that money available to the population served by an authority is fixed. Therefore the more money that is given to a total purchasing pilot, the less is available for the rest of the population, and vice versa.

Getting this right is crucial. The consideration of historic and capitation budgets and their calculation follow.

Historic budgets

An historic budget is calculated by multiplying all of the activity for patients served by a total purchasing pilot by the cost of that activity. While this seems a straightforward calculation, the difficulties soon reveal themselves once the process is started.

The first problem is to determine precisely what the activity was. Health service data from providers are neither complete nor totally accurate. This is because information systems were, in the past, never designed for use in a 'market setting'. Substantial improvements (through substantial investment) have occurred, particularly in the past three years. However, no provider will have 100% accuracy. Providing excellent data costs money, and there inevitably has to be a compromise between the ideal and the reasonable. The result is that some activity in providers remains unrecorded, there is duplication in recording and coding (clinical and nonclinical) has errors and omissions.

The same complications also apply to costing the activity, but perhaps even more so. The sophistication of most health service contracts in terms of pricing is low. Most providers are highly complex organizations providing a huge variety of services in a flexible way to individual patients. Providing realistic costs for these services is an immense task, especially since there was little need to cost any services in detail before the introductions of the internal market. Again the situation has improved, and most provider contracts will have at least prices at a specialty level and may have different prices for inpatient, day case, emergency, elective and outpatient activity. However, few would believe that these prices are the true cost of this activity. This view is reinforced by the substantial price shifts between costs of activity within providers from year to year, and price variation between providers (and even between purchasers for the same provider).

These price fluctuations within a provider mean that historic budgets based on previous year's prices run the risk of being too low or too high to support the activity. On the other hand a budget set on next year's price shields the total purchasing project from overall price rises of providers above the level of inflation.

The purpose of raising these difficulties of historic budget calculation is not to dismiss this method as a reasonable method for budget calculation. It does have the advantages that, at least superficially, it is easy to understand, produces a budget that reflects past demand for health services and should not produce early winners or losers in allocations. Whatever method of budget setting is decided upon, it is sensible to calculate current expenditure as a baseline measure so that everyone knows what they may be letting themselves in for at the start.

Capitation budgets

At its simplest a capitation budget would give the total purchasing project a sum of money for each registered patient. However, the needs for health services are not uniform across all age groups and sections of society. In general the older people are, the more likely they are to be sick (although there is obviously a big demand put on health services at the time of birth and in the neonatal period), and similarly the poor tend to be ill more often than the rich. GP populations are not identical, so a budget based simply on practice list size would produce profound inequalities in provision.

To cope with this, the amount of money can be varied to account for interpractice variation in age, sex and social conditions, giving a 'weighted' capitation budget. Exactly how this should be done is itself more problematical. However, it is far from a new problem and has been the subject of much research and political debate.

When the NHS was established in 1948, it pulled together existing services that had been provided to varying levels in different parts of the country. In the 1970s the government tried to bring greater equity to health service funding between regions by the development of a capitation formula rather than simply reflecting the historic patterns. A formula, known as the RAWP formula after the Regional Allocation Working Party that devised it, gave a different weight to age groups and an adjustment for need (through the use of the standardized mortality ratio: SMR). As with all such formulae a balance had to be struck between complexity and ability to calculate – particularly through the use of routinely available data. The use of the formula gave a target proportion of allocation to each RHA, to which each has moved closer over time.

A revised formula for allocation of budgets between RHAs in England was devised in 1994 by the Centre for Health Economics at York University and implemented in the financial year 1995/6. RHAs have in turn used the formula to allocate resources to districts. Like the old RAWP formula this new one, commonly called the York formula, gives a different weighting for different age groups and an adjustment for need. Its calculation is, however, much more complex, in that the adjustment for need not only includes the SMR but also several indicators of deprivation derived from the national census.

Process of calculating a capitation budget for a total purchasing project

The following is a description of the process by which a capitation budget for a total purchasing project can be calculated. The endpoint is a percentage share of the allocation given to the health authority.

Population in age bands

The first part of the calculation involves determining the number of people in the area served by the authority as a whole and those served by the total purchasing pilot. Furthermore, this population needs to be broken down into a number of age bands. The most obvious place to get these data from is the database of patients registered with GPs (usually called the FHSA register). Technically this is a very easy task, but one should bear the following in mind.

1 The register usually has more people on it than actually live within an area served. The extent of this inflation of list size is variable in different parts of the country and between practices. Practices that have spent effort on removing such 'ghosts' from lists will therefore be disadvantaged.

2 Patients living within an authority's area may be registered with GPs outside this area. It is therefore important to ensure that data from those patients are collected by liaison with neighbouring authorities.

3 Not all people within an authority's boundary are registered with a GP. Allowance has to be made for this in setting the budget, as if all money went to GPs the authority would be left with no money to pay for their patients. (An alternative is to charge the total purchasing pilot its capitation share, in year, of the cost of activity provided for unregistered patients.)

Births

The York formula (and previous RAWP) gives an additional weighting for births. The FHSA register does not currently record that a new registration is because of a birth. However, an estimate can be made by assuming that all new registrations below the age of one year are births.

Deprivation weighting

The York formula for allocation has a weighting to take account of population need. This deprivation weight is a composite of a number of variables that are collected as part of the census together with the SMR for deaths of people under 75 years of age. The most obvious problem in calculating a budget for a total purchasing pilot is that it is impossible to link these factors directly to general practice populations, as neither the census nor death certificates record GPs. A way around this is instead to link the practice populations to local authority wards, for which both SMR and census data are easily obtainable.

To illustrate this, and the underlying assumptions that go with it, imagine that you want to estimate the number of deaths for a particular GP practice.

Using the FHSA database it is possible to find out for any given ward the number of patients (in each age band if needed) who are registered with each GP. For simplicity let us say that one quarter are with GP A, three-quarters with GP B and none registered with any other GP. Now from the Office of Population Censuses and Surveys (OPCS) it is possible to get the number of deaths that have occurred in that ward, by age group and sex, within a calendar year. Let us say that for the particular ward in question this is 20. One can then make a simple assumption that the populations served by the GPs A and B are the same in every way in that ward. Therefore the number of deaths for GP A in the ward can be estimated as 5 and for B 15. By repeating this process for every ward, it is then possible to estimate all the deaths from all GPs.

The assumption that the patients on the list of different GPs are identical is of course unlikely to be true. It is also probably true, in general, that the larger the ward, the less likely the assumption is to be true; however, pragmatically there is little else one can do. A greater degree of sophistication is to decrease the size of the geographical area. This is possible, and census data can certainly be obtained for very small areas (around 150 households). However, the task of allocating the variable to each GP becomes computationally much more onerous.

In a similar way for estimating deaths by GP, the census data can be used to calculate a deprivation score for each GP and thus a total purchasing pilot.

As stated at the beginning of this section, the end result of this process should be a proportionate share of the health authority allocation for buying services. This is the beginning of the process. The authority and the total purchasing pilot will need to agree in detail issues such as money for top slices (national, regional and local) and services that the total purchasing pilot will be buying, and the acceptability of risk. Fundholding budgets for the practices involved will need to be subtracted from the capitation budget.

Accountability

Total purchasing gives GPs much greater power over what services to buy and how these services are delivered. However, power should carry with it greater responsibility and accountability. Therefore to whom are GPs participating in total purchasing accountable, and by what mechanism? This is a vexed question and still really to be resolved. At the moment accountability for purchasing of services (including staying within budget) and improving health of the population served by total purchasing remains with the health authority. Therefore there is a tension for the authority in its desire to give the total purchasing pilot freedom to make choices and have power while actually being responsible for those choices.

There is no simple answer to resolve this dilemma. Total purchasing pilots and authorities both need to recognize it and work together to ensure that problems are minimized. Part of this is that the expectation of what will be achieved by total purchasing is clear. This should take the form of a 'contract' between the authority and the GPs. This contract should include financial monitoring and rules, delivery of national and locally agreed policy, information reporting and improvement of population health.

Benefits and costs – lessons from one year's experience in Berkshire

The participation in the total purchasing pilot has produced many benefits to Berkshire Health Authority. In particular it has gained the experience of working with a large number of GPs, which will be invaluable for its future plans to move to locality working throughout the county. The authority is now much clearer about how this should work (and the benefits and risks of the process). The clear benefit for the authority is to have GPs responsible for the health services they demand for their population in terms of their resource consequences and the effectiveness of these services to deliver benefit.

The main cost to the authority has been its staff time. A significant proportion of its senior staff has been involved in the total purchasing project, with the result that they have had less time to devolve to other aspects of the authority's work.

3

The total purchasing group – relations between individual GPs, practices and the health authority

Rod Smith

Most total purchasing pilots involve several practices in order to reduce the risk inherent in purchasing care for small populations. Risk management is an important area for all total purchasing pilots to consider, particularly those with very small populations, usually single practices. The disciplines of total purchasing are somewhat different from standard fundholding as practices are sharing the new part of the budget and will need to consider carefully what arrangements they will come to in the event of over- or underspends.

Legislation does not allow total purchasers to have a complete budget in their own right, so the most common arrangement is for a capitation budget to be set for the whole group, and for individual practice fundholding budgets to be set in the usual way by the health authority, as applied to all fundholders, and to be top-sliced from the capitation budget.

The new part of the budget is controlled by the total purchasing group, acting as a sub-committee of the health authority, who will want to see robust monitoring arrangements in place to ensure financial control and probity.

Capitation budgets may prove difficult to set for individual practices or groups of practices (see Chapter 2 for more detail). In theory they should be set in the same way as for the health authority using the York formula, but this may prove difficult as practices often straddle several wards and the formula was not in any case developed to be used for such small populations as a single practice. A further problem is that well-established fundholding practices may well start off more efficient in terms of low referral rates, etc. than the rest of the authority practices; thus a capitation formula may produce a higher budget than an historic resource usage formula produces. Where pilots start off with a higher historic spend than the capitation formula produces, authorities will rightly be cautious about giving practices a higher proportion of the authority's resources than fairness decrees. Fundholders will be extremely cautious about accepting historic hospital and community service data, the collection of which has not been disciplined by fundholder practice validation, as experience within fundholding has taught us that data are not always accurately collected, particularly where there have been no financial consequences to poor collection (there are of course within fundholding). Agreement will need to be reached with the health authority on how to deal with any discrepancy between capitation and historic budgets.

The relationship between the new budget and practice fundholding budgets

Most practices will want to continue managing their own fundholding budget within the practice as they will have developed different priorities over the years, which they will wish to maintain. Expenditure within fundholding over £6000 will need to be recovered from the new part of the budget, as will any overspends by individual practices.

Total purchasing pilots will need to agree with their health authorities how to deal with overspends of the total budget, and this may depend on how the budget was set. If the total budget was set using a capitation formula, it would seem inappropriate to expect the health authority to bail out an overspend, so in Berkshire we have agreed that in-year fundholding savings will be the first call on overspends. Careful monitoring is required to ensure that we are not heading for an overspend, and we have agreed to slow elective surgery first before, as a final resort, going to the health authority for more resources. If a total purchasing pilot needed to be rescued from an overspend by its authority, a move that would consequently take resources away from patients of other GPs, careful examination of the reasons and an action plan to bring the total purchasing group's spending into line with the rest of the health authority would need to be developed. Where the budget had been set on historic data that produced a lower budget than would a capitation formula, it would seem appropriate for the health authority to cover overspends up to the level of the capitation share of the total purchasing pilot.

Relations between practices

Total purchasing pilots involving several practices vary widely in how much they have worked together before: some will have worked together in fundholding consortia or night co-operatives, whereas others may simply be GPs in the same area who have expressed an interest in total purchasing. Some will form natural localities, enhancing joint innovation, whereas others will be more geographically spread. Some will use deputizing services while others will do their own on-call (use of deputizing services may increase admissions). Practices will inevitably have different referral and resource usage patterns. Discussion will need to take place on how to deal with individual practice overspends. If the whole project is heading for an underspend, there will clearly be less of a problem than if it is heading for an overspend and fundholding budgets are being called on from underspending practices.

At least one total purchasing project has devolved budgets direct to its practices. In Berkshire we have not done this but are monitoring each practice's expenditure and encouraging practices to work within their budget.

The BIPP monitors expenditure in the following categories:

- main hospital contract

    - inpatients
    - outpatients
    - pathology (block)

- community and mental health Trust, including new community beds

- external contracts (purchased through the health authority)

- ECRs

- ambulance reserve (a new fund for GPs to use ambulances for transport to the surgery rather than hospital)

- nursing reserve (a new fund to enable GPs to use night agency nurses to keep patients out of hospital)

- innovation fund (capitation fund averaging about £10 000 per practice for practices to develop services as alternatives to hospital usage, for example a nurse on all day to see casualties, or an occupational therapist to expedite early discharges).

The ECR information is particularly useful as it allows local gaps in service to be identified and whether to encourage providers to develop new services to be considered.

For each of these categories a spend for each practice for year to date and projected annual spend can be identified and fed to practices.

As total purchasing pilots develop it may be possible to devolve total budgets into individual practices, but until the full nature of risk is understood it is probably safer for the new part of the budget to be pooled.

Creating ownership of decision making by individual GPs

Pooling budgets between several practices makes it more difficult for total purchasing pilots to create incentives for individual GPs to change their behaviour. Within a fundholding practice efficiency savings from reduced referrals or provision of a psychologist or counsellor within the practice can be rapidly invested in reduced waiting times or a new practice service. Even though the GP may need to work harder, he or she at least sees very rapid patient benefits. In a group of practices efficiency savings made by one practice might need to be invested in another practice's overspend, and change is inevitably more bureaucratic to achieve. Practices need to be given incentives to be efficient; one way to achieve this is to give practices an innovation fund to allow them to develop their own interests. This can only be done when the project managers are confident that the necessary resources are available, using either growth money (where it exists) or efficiency savings. Practice innovations may lead to further efficiency savings, for example an extra practice nurse to reduce A&E usage or an evening family planning nurse to reduce more expensive community clinic usage. As the project approaches year end and financial data are firmed up, more resources may be released for innovation, but projects will need to exercise caution about making long-term commitments for future years unless they are confident of both future funding and their ability to continue to make efficiency savings to support a long-term commitment.

Total purchasing projects and strategic development

Total purchasing requires a more strategic approach to purchasing than does standard fundholding. To fulfil the maximum potential of total purchasing requires a merging of the tactical skills that fundholding has used to effect change with the longer-term strategic skills that health authorities possess. Total purchasing projects must work closely with their health authority. In a primary care-led NHS the local strategic framework should be a joint development between all GPs, including total purchasers, so if the health authority has properly involved all GPs the total purchasing group should have little difficulty in signing up to the health authority's strategy. If the total purchasing pilot is working well, it may be in a better position than the authority itself to delivery strategic change as change often requires resources – for example doing more work in primary care requires extra resources – which fundholders can produce through efficiency savings. Many authorities find it difficult to encourage non-fundholding GPs to change, as there are no real incentives for them to do so and lack of freed-up resources has often made strategic change difficult to implement. Many GPs have grown cynical about talk of work and resources moving into primary care with little practical evidence of this happening, except through fundholding. Other major strategic changes, such as closure of an old-fashioned mental health hospital, may require extra resources during the transition period to a new mental health core unit and additional community mental health services. Total purchasing pilots will need to appraise themselves of major strategic changes planned, be involved in their development and consider how they will find the resources from their purchasing budgets to fund extra expenditure arising from them.

The role of the lead GP and fund manager in total purchasing

The involvement of a lead GP and fund manager from each practice is essential (see Chapter 6). Their role is to liaise with the rest of the practices, the project manager and the health authority, and be involved in the development of a purchasing policy for the project. They also need to consider carefully how to involve partners within their practices in the project. Contracting will be much more successful if GPs and consultants are involved in the contracting process. GP, fund manager and clerical assistant's time will need to be paid for, and the current additional management allowance from the NHS Executive will probably be inadequate to cover the extra costs. Initially at least total purchasing management costs will be additional to authority management costs; indeed the authority's costs may rise as a result of total purchasing as invoices sent to the authority need to be disaggregated to the correct authority budget, total purchasing group or rest of authority group (distant Trusts will be unaware of the existence of a local total purchasing pilot and will invoice the health authority). Over time and as authorities devolve their staff to locality purchasing groups, it should be possible for authority management costs to be devolved to the localities. A successful total purchasing pilot will hopefully provide the model and expertise for locality purchasing. In the meantime total purchasing projects will have to obtain management resources from a combination of the NHS Executive management allowance, whatever resources their health authority can afford to release from their overall management costs, and efficiency savings from their agreed capitation budget. In the long term total purchasing will only be viable if management costs are lower than existing management costs of authorities or if it is able to demonstrate an improved delivery of health care.

Relations with the health authority

The close involvement of GPs with their health authority is a vital ingredient for success in total purchasing. Both parties have much to gain from a positive relationship. Fundholders bring experience of high-quality information gathering, an ability to achieve rapid tactical change and an ability to involve all GPs in the search for efficiency savings, while authorities bring their long experience of strategic change, public health skills and knowledge of areas of health care of which GPs have little experience such as dentistry and the risk management of high-cost, low-volume procedures, for example bone marrow transplants and forensic psychiatry.

Dealing with overspends and underspends (savings)

In the Berkshire total purchasing project there appeared to be a gap between the historic consumption of resources by the six practices and the figure produced by a capitation formula. This presented considerable problems to both parties as the original agreement had been that BIPP should have a capitation budget, and the GPs were reluctant to accept the accuracy of historic data. Eventually agreement was reached that 30% of the gap should be held in a buffer fund, which could be used by the practices if needed. The GPs would not have been willing to use their potential fundholding savings to bail out an overspend without a fair capitation budget. The buffer fund would be returned to the health authority as soon as it was clear that the project could manage without it. Further agreement was reached that savings on the new part of the budget would be capped at 1%; anything greater would be returned to the health authority.

Restrictions were also put on the use of savings with the agreement of the NHS Executive:

BIPP funds may be used for the full range of services covered by Hospital and Community Health Services and GP fundholding scheme as agreed by the purchasing forum, within NHS policies. The purchase of equipment or Health Promotion materials will need the prior approval of the Health Commission. BIPP savings will not be used for the purchase or extension of buildings.

Overspends are potentially more difficult. Providing a capitation budget has been agreed, the authors believe it is right that the first call for an overspend should be on potential fundholding savings of participating practices, as it would be inequitable for the health authority to use the resources of patients of GPs outside the pilot. Where a budget lower than capitation has been agreed, it would seem equitable to make the authority responsible for overspends up to the capitation level, and then the fundholding savings. If a total purchasing pilot needs further resources than capitation share or overspends its capitation budget, other GPs in the authority's areas might legitimately challenge whether the pilot should continue.

Accountability

Standard fundholders are accountable to the NHS Executive, through NHS Executive regional offices, although in practice day-to-day accountability is to the local health authority. Practices within total purchasing pilots remain accountable for their standard fundholding responsibilities in the same way as all standard fundholders and have four main areas of accountability:

1 management accountability

2 accountability to patients and the wider public

3 financial accountability

4 clinical and professional accountability.

Accountability for the new non-fundholding part of the fund will be to the health authority, as the total purchasing pilot is essentially a health authority sub-committee. There are no additional national accountability requirements, but the health authority will clearly want to put robust accountability arrangements in place, building on standard fundholding arrangements. Key requirements for the standard fundholder are outlined in Box 3.1.

Formal discussion and a written agreement between the GPs and the health authority will help to clarify the responsibilities of each party. The

Box 3.1: Key requirements for standard fundholder

Management accountability

- Preparation of an annual practice plan
- Signalling major shifts in purchasing intentions
- Preparation of an annual performance report
- Review performance with the health authority within the national framework

Accountability to patients and the wider public

- Publishing information, e.g. annual practice plan and performance report
- Involve patients in service planning
- Ensure an effective complaints system

Financial accountability

- Preparation of annual accounts for independent audit
- Provide monthly information for monitoring by the health authority
- Securing agreement to proposed use of savings for material or equipment purchases (including those relating to health education), improvement of premises, clinical audit, research and training
- Stating planned contribution to the local efficiency targets set by the NHS Executive

Clinical and professional accountability

- Participating in clinical audit of GMS activities
- Ensuring that agreed audit programmes are completed by hospital and community health care service providers

following represents a suggested structure for formal agreement in drawing up an agreement between the health authority and GPs.

Section 1 – Introduction

- Purpose of project
- Financial management and controls
- Efficiency index target

Section 2 – Accountability, relationship with fundholding and definitions

- Constitution and responsibilities of purchasing forum
- Budget setting arrangements
- Alignment of purchasing strategy with authorities
- Contract monitoring arrangements
- ECR authorization procedures
- Relationship with fundholding, including need to call on fundholding savings to fund overspends
- Definition of patient population (including proportional share of expenditure on patients not registered with a GP)

Section 3 – Financial arrangements

- Need to follow health authority's standing financial instructions
- Recognition that authority director of finance is ultimately responsible for total purchasing project expenditure
- Funding arrangements including:
    - top-sliced items, e.g. authority administrative costs
    - levies: funds deducted for national/regional requirements, e.g. Section 64 grants to hospices; genitourinary medicine, special health authority contracts
    - fundholding budgets, expenditure over £6000 per individual patient and fundholding practice overspend
    - certain agreed blocked-back funds for the authority to purchase services to an agreed level for project, e.g. clinical audit, bone marrow transplants and community dental funds. Even though

these are blocked back to the authority, the project is responsible for over- or underspends

- project's discretionary funds to cover contracts made exclusively by the total purchasing project:

  (i) funds for the main provider hospital
  (ii) funds for the main community Trust
  (iii) funds for ECRs
  (iv) funds for small-volume providers negotiated on behalf of project by the health authority to an agreed level

- Audit requirements

- Financial strategy and agreement to manage within agreed budget

- Use of savings

- Monthly financial reporting

- Agreement to validate invoices

Section 4 – Purchasing arrangements

- Agreement to contribute to authority's corporate contract targets, including efficiency index

- Agreement to supply authority with a purchasing plan

- Agreement on external contracts to be covered by the health authority

- Risk sharing arrangements

- ECR management

- Agreement to abide by authority's purchasing strategy (e.g. *in vitro* fertilization treatment not being purchased) unless divergence from the strategy is agreed with the health authority

Section 5 – Monitoring arrangements

- Monthly reports to purchasing forum, including all directly negotiated contracts and those negotiated by the health authority

- Quarterly performance review by the health authority

- Agreement to help the health authority resolve complaints from patients, their families, members of the public and MPs.

4

Project management

Fran Butler

Setting up and developing a total purchasing scheme can at first appear daunting. There are many different parties involved (practices, providers and the health authority); it is not immediately clear what the role of each is, how they should relate to each other, what the key activities are in order to prepare for and run the scheme, or who should be responsible for driving the scheme forward. The purpose of this chapter is to address some of these issues and highlight some of the pitfalls to avoid in taking total purchasing forward. The chapter is based mainly on experiences in Berkshire but is of general relevance. Advice generally refers to multi-practice projects and would need to be modified for projects involving only one practice.

The Berkshire project was set up using a modified version of PRINCE (PRojects IN Controlled Environment), a formal method widely used in the health service for managing projects. PRINCE provides the necessary framework to define, manage and control projects. The GPs were at first a little bemused by this approach, but several have since mentioned how useful they have found the structure, particularly in the reporting of progress against plan. In particular, the project initiation document, a central feature of PRINCE, ensured that fundamentals such as scope, project funding and plans were agreed and documented at the outset.

Establishing the objectives

Before all else those involved in the project should consider what they hope to achieve from it; the aims and objectives of the project should be clearly defined and documented. There is a danger with any project, particularly one as complicated in its operation as a total purchasing scheme, that the processes of operating the project, collecting and validating information, and negotiating and managing contracts become all-consuming, and that those involved can lose sight of the original reasons for initiating the scheme. It is also possible that some practices may have embarked on total purchasing without a clear idea of what they wanted to achieve, and the task of documenting the aims and objectives will help to focus minds and ensure that all parties are working towards the same goals. At this point basic differences in motivation and expectation among practices, or between practices and the health authority, may be revealed, which are best resolved early one.

By way of an example, there had been an underlying tension in the Berkshire project between the health authority and the GPs about the budget-setting process and the extent of freedom being offered to the GPs in the use of the budget. The health authority also had objectives contained in the corporate contract agreed with the regional office, but the GPs had strong objections to signing up to some of these (in particular the efficiency index targets, which would have operated against reducing emergencies). These differences were only resolved shortly before the start of the live year, in the meantime leaving all parties in some doubt as to whether the project would proceed.

Documented objectives can be referred to as the project progresses, to serve as a check that the project is heading in the right direction to achieve them, and to assess whether they require updating in the light of events.

The purpose and objectives of the BIPP scheme were as follows.

Purpose
To inform the development of purchasing within the NHS by combining GP fundholding and health authority skills, with the aim of purchasing more effective and responsive health care across the whole range of services for the population covered.

Objectives

- To establish the feasibility of local purchasing led by GPs within an agreed strategic framework and to provide experience for the health authority and GP fundholders for future locality purchasing.

- To bring fundholder knowledge of patients to bear to improve non-fund-holding services, including:

  - reducing inpatient admissions and length of stay where appropriate
  - bringing non-inpatient services closer to the patient
  - reviewing A&E service provision with the aim of providing a more cost effective and appropriate service
  - reviewing provision of patient transport services with the aim of providing a more effective and appropriate service
  - postponing need for residential care thereby enabling people to stay in their own homes longer

- developing relationships with social services and other relevant agencies at local level
- making other changes as identified by purchasing forum.

- To investigate and attempt to explain rises in numbers of emergency admissions, and to cope with these risks.

- To improve integration of primary and secondary health care, and make appropriate shifts of provision from secondary to primary health care services.

- To provide the most cost effective purchasing, with the aim of freeing resources which can be used to improve patterns of care delivery.

- To assess management requirements (including those of providers) for contracting at local level, and to assess whether the benefits of purchasing in this way outweigh these management costs.

The emphasis is on purchasing health care effectively to maximize benefits to patients from the finite resources available.

The stated purpose of the project reflects to some extent that BIPP was one of the original four national projects and obtained national funding; projects setting up now might have a stated purpose with a more locally oriented flavour.

In clarifying objectives it may become clear that the practices involved are only interested in making changes in a very few services, for example maternity or emergency admissions in particular specialties, requiring a minimal infrastructure for the project and no additional staff. It is therefore vital that the objectives are developed before proceeding to make decisions about the project organization or funding requirements.

Project organization

The BIPP organizational structure and accountabilities are summarized in Figure 4.1. The diagram looks complicated at first glance but shows how the two main bodies and the sub-groups relate to each other. Such a structure was felt to be necessary to ensure that the appropriate input was made to all project decisions and in determining project direction. The two main groups are:

1 the project board – the steering group for the project

2 the purchasing forum, where the purchasing direction and day-to-day decisions are determined.

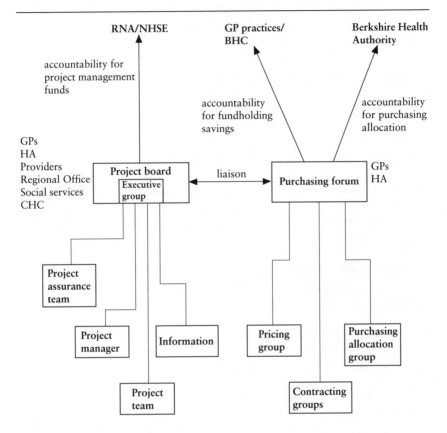

Figure 4.1: The project organizational structure.

The project board

Because of the scope and impact of the project, the usual PRINCE guidelines regarding the project board were stretched (perhaps beyond recognition), particularly with respect to the number of representatives and the frequency of meetings.

The project board is the key decision making and steering body, and is responsible for overseeing progress and ensuring that the project as far as possible meets its objectives. It is not responsible for purchasing decisions; these are the responsibility of the purchasing forum (see page 28). The board consists of representatives from all involved organizations, namely:

- the six practices (a GP from each and also a couple of fund managers)

- Berkshire Health Authority

- Royal Berkshire and Battle Hospitals Trust
- West Berkshire Priority Care Services NHS Trust
- Royal Berkshire Ambulance NHS Trust
- Anglia and Oxford Regional Office
- Berkshire Social Services
- West Berkshire Community Health Council.

The Board is chaired by a GP. A smaller executive group (a sub-set of the project board) was identified, consisting of only one representative from each organization, to enable the project manager to obtain decisions or advice on certain project matters without having to consult the entire board.

Many total purchasing projects have steering groups that consist wholly of practice and health authority representatives. BIPP has found the presence of the other organizations on the board to be extremely beneficial. In particular, the presence of providers and social services has ensured their involvement in the decision making process relating to the non-purchasing aspects of the project. GPs in particular were keen to involve providers, as their experience was that providers were not fully prepared for fundholding.

On the downside, focused decision making and steering of the project can often be difficult, given the large number of players present at meetings and the different interests of the organizations they represent.

It is of interest to note that at least one total purchasing scheme has a patient on the project board.

Purchasing forum

The purchasing forum is responsible for the purchasing and contracting aspects of the project, including remaining with the purchasing budget. The group consists of one GP from each of the participating practices, four health authority representatives (one from each of the information, finance, public health and purchasing directorates) and the project manager. There is no provider representation on the purchasing forum, although there is provider involvement in sub-groups set up by the forum, and provider representatives are sometimes invited to speak at meetings of the forum. Following legal advice with respect to accountability, the purchasing forum was made a sub-committee of the health authority board.

The full terms of reference for the purchasing forum are given in Appendix 2.

The project board and purchasing forum both meet monthly. Additionally the BIPP GPs meet together at a separate monthly meeting to discuss clinical issues relating to the project.

Funding

Funding was obtained from the NHS Executive and from Anglia and Oxford RHA for practices, the health authority, and the two main providers, for administrative staff to support the project (and in the case of practices for locum support). It is recognized that the level of funding was influenced by the project's position as one of the first pilots, and that subsequent pilots received less. All organizations involved need to consider the resource implications of being involved in a total purchasing scheme, although they will need to acknowledge that the ideal level of funding is unlikely to be available.

Administrative base

If a project has more than one practice, an administrative base will need to be chosen to provide a focal point for the co-ordination, administration and contract monitoring functions. This might be based at one of the practices or at the health authority.

The project manager role

To drive forward and co-ordinate the project, the appointment of a project manager is essential. In defining the nature of the post or role, the following should be considered.

To whom should the project manager be accountable?

In some total purchasing schemes, the project manager is accountable only to the GPs and not to the health authority. In Berkshire the project manager is accountable to the project board, in practice reporting mainly to the GPs but also in part to the health authority. It is important that the project manager enjoys the confidence of both, regardless of accountabilities – the GPs because they need to be able to concentrate on their clinical responsibilities in the knowledge that the project is being well run, and the health authority because it must be happy that the project has been set up in a way that will support tight contract and financial control.

How much project manager effort is required?

This will depend on the role to be played, how many practices are involved and whether there are any support staff. The Berkshire project manager is full time. In projects with only one or two practices, a fund manager may be able to fill the project manager role, although this will require additional working hours.

What skills, knowledge and qualities are required?

A project manager of a total purchasing scheme requires knowledge of most aspects of health service purchasing, including contracting, information, finance and fundholding, and also project management experience. In practice it may not be possible to recruit someone with experience of all of these, but in-depth experience of one or more areas plus the ability to learn quickly is essential. Provision of support in particular areas can reduce the expertise directly required by the project manager.

The project manager needs to have the ability to place a structure around the various activities required and make them happen, some by delegation and some by carrying them out personally.

Co-ordinating GPs has been described as being like herding cats; therefore the project manager also needs to be an effective 'cat herder' (Figure 4.2).

Key tasks of the total purchasing scheme project manager

The project manager's activities differ greatly between the preparatory year and live year. The preparatory year is taken up with organizing the set-up of the infrastructure for purchasing and contract management and monitoring, while the live year is much more concerned with the practice of contract management, monitoring and giving feedback to GPs both on a macro contract level and an individual patient level.

Key tasks for the preparatory year

The purpose of the preparatory year is to ensure that live running commences on a sound basis, and in particular with the best possible estimate of likely expenditure on services. A good knowledge of historical

ESF. 95.

Figure 4.2: Trying to co-ordinate GPs is like herding cats.

purchasing, both its nature and its cost, will allow GPs to take informed purchasing decisions in terms of benefit to patients and remaining within budget.

The preparatory year needs planning, so in ideal circumstances the project should be started, with the project manager in post, prior to this. In particular detailed information will need to be collected by providers from 1 April of that year, and work on the purchasing intentions must be sufficiently advanced by the end of September to allow any intended major shifts to be notified to providers at that time.

A checklist of the preparatory year tasks for practices and the authority is given in Appendix 1. The key tasks are to:

- develop the purchasing plan, including some needs assessment and looking at risk management

- liaise with providers about intended service changes and price structures
- develop procedures for contract management
- develop ECR protocols
- develop other protocols where required, for example for admissions to community hospitals
- calculate purchasing allocation (an authority responsibility; see Chapter 2)
- formalize arrangements between authority and practices about key responsibilities and accountability
- monitor shadow contracts against a shadow budget
- decide how to involve patients and the public in general
- document information requirements (see Chapter 7)
- procure and implement information system (if required – see Chapter 7)
- negotiate contracts.

A successful preparatory year is necessary for successful live operation. The more that the live year can be mimicked in the preparatory year (for instance by validating provider data and by shadow monitoring of contracts), the better the footing for live operation, and the less of the live year or years that will be taken up in the learning process.

Key tasks for live working

From the GPs' point of view, once the project is live they are able to put into practice changes that they have been planning. In Berkshire, for instance, this meant that new GP beds were now available at a local community hospital. Protocols for patient care may need revising in the light of experience.

Information received from providers should be analysed to provide GPs with greater detail about purchased activity. In-year developments for providing different and better care can flow from such analyses. Examples of these are given in Chapter 7.

The administrative procedures developed during the preparatory year will take time to settle down and should be continually reviewed. It is important to note that the ECR procedures need to be introduced before the start of the live year in order to ensure that the authority does not authorize ECRs that may be due to take place in the live year.

Validation by the practices needs to begin, and contract monitoring is possible, once data begin to flow in from providers. Initial monitoring reports will be awaited eagerly, but expenditure on emergency admissions and ECRs can fluctuate significantly from month to month, and it is important not to panic or be lulled into a false sense of security by one or two months' figures.

As the new contracting year begins, there is a temptation to breathe a sigh of relief that the hard work of contract negotiations is over. Beware of any temptation to relax – this is the time to start work on next year's purchasing plan!

The purchasing plan

The process for developing a purchasing plan will vary from project to project and will depend on the number of practices involved and the relationship with the health authority. In Berkshire the purchasing forum led this process, and decisions were made mostly by the GPs, with advice from the health authority. The description that follows relates to the *process* of developing the plan; the strategic considerations surrounding purchasing are covered in Chapter 5.

Total purchasing schemes should discuss with their health authority whether adherence to health authority policies is required (e.g. whether to purchase *in vitro* fertilization, tattoo removal, etc.). This may be a highly contentious issue. In Berkshire the GPs recognized the potential undesired consequences of divergence and have agreed that health authority policies will be adhered to except by prior agreement, if necessary of the health authority board.

A full list of services purchased by the authority can be drawn up, and the services can then be categorized as follows:

- those to be purchased directly by the project with changes to services
- those to be purchased directly by the project with no change
- those to be purchased via the authority on an actual usage basis
- those to be purchased via the authority on a capitation percentage basis.

The project's main priorities for change in year one were identified as emergency admissions, GP beds at a community hospital, the A&E service and family planning. Pace of change was wholly dependent on information availability for the latter two services; this is covered in more detail in Chapter 7.

About 90% of BIPP activity was taking place at the two local providers – Royal Berkshire and Battle Hospitals NHS Trust and West Berkshire Priority Care Services NHS Trust. A decision was therefore taken that BIPP would have its own contracts at these providers but that Berkshire health authority would purchase activity on behalf of BIPP for the specialist work at other providers. This has so far worked well in practice and has allowed the GPs to concentrate on local priorities while avoiding ECR prices at these providers.

Some other work is purchased via the health authority because of difficulties in disaggregating or because the work is not specifically patient based. Examples include health promotion and school nursing, where the project pays a capitation percentage of the cost of the service. Consideration of purchasing risks, in particular low-incidence, high-cost activity, may result in the decision to purchase yet other services via the health authority.

If there is to be a significant change for any one provider as a result of any total purchasing initiatives, major shifts must be notified, normally by the end of September of the year before. It is important to find out from the regional office the precise rules about major shifts, including the definition and how to notify them, and to adhere to these rules. Major shifts not notified correctly may not be allowed, and a whole year will then pass before the planned change can be made.

Although purchasing plans will be drawn up once a year, the contents, including needs assessment for practice populations and service reviews, will be the result of a whole year's work. Additionally assessment of referral and activity patterns and resultant decisions should be a continual process, as many changes can be made in-year within existing contracts.

Developing administrative procedures

1 *Contract management* – procedures should identify responsibilities of the different parties. They describe how data flow to practices from local providers (directly) and from external providers (via the health authority), how the data should be validated, how errors should be reported and how the contract monitoring reports are to be prepared.

2 *External contracts* – these procedures should define how the contracts will be managed on behalf of the project, and how decisions will be

reached about the level of payment to be made to the health authority for project patient activity.

3 *ECRs* – ECR procedures will need to identify the flow of paperwork between practices and the health authority 'safe haven', and the means by which ECRs will be authorized (see below).

4 *Financial* – these procedures should state how the project budget is identified within the authority's systems, how internal payments are to be made, how invoices should be processed and any reports required by the health authority.

As a whole these procedures define the way in which practices, the health authority and the project's administrative office will work together in an administrative sense. Their drawing-up will require the co-operation of all parties. The health authority should not underestimate the amount of work involved for its staff in having a total purchasing project in its patch.

Managing ECRs

Managing ECRs within a total purchasing scheme, as within a health authority, has two aspects to it. The project needs to decide how these will be managed.

Clinical

GPs need to be involved in deciding whether individual ECRs will be authorized in cases where the purchaser has discretion. In Berkshire whether an ECR is authorized or not is decided at the purchasing forum by GPs on a majority vote basis. The public health representative on the purchasing forum should play a vital role in advising on effectiveness, possible alternative providers and possible political consequences of refusal. The resulting decision is often that the GP will go back and speak to the patient to discuss an alternative approach advised by the forum.

Experience to date has shown the discussions in the purchasing forum to be an extremely constructive way of dealing with ECR authorizations, and the GPs have, if anything, been more selective than the health authority in these decisions.

Administrative

The BIPP office works very closely with the health authority ECR 'safe haven', as most ECR communication is initially directed there. The 'safe haven' staff are a source of very useful information with respect to ECR regulations. ECR minimum data sets (MDSs) are validated by practices and ECR invoices paid only on the agreement of the practice.

Experience to date

A successful project depends on having an appropriate project structure to suit local circumstances, in particular to ensure that all necessary parties are suitably involved. Experience in Berkshire has shown that there are benefits from involving providers in the steering forum, although their presence in discussing purchasing matters, except by invitation, is inappropriate.

Time spent identifying the deliverables for the preparatory year and live year, and in working out procedures detailing how the different parties will work together, is time well invested. Problems experienced in Berkshire mostly arose where particular deliverables (e.g. the purchasing budget and the agreement between GPs and the health authority) were delayed, leaving little time to resolve differences through unpressured debate before the live year began.

Because total purchasing projects are using part of the health authority budget, and because their purchasing is officially health authority purchasing, close working with the health authority is essential regardless of the siting of the project's administrative base.

5

Contracting for change
Rod Smith

The purchasing forum

A key task for a total purchasing project is to set up a body to make purchasing or commissioning decisions. This will be easiest in a single practice, where the partners and fund manager, together with one or more representatives from the health authority, will probably be the purchasing forum. In a larger group involving several practices, the purchasing forum will need to have a representative from each practice, public health and health authority finance and/or commissioning personnel and the project manager. Frequency of meetings needs to be decided by the group but will need to be at least monthly and probably more frequently.

There needs to be clarity about the powers of the purchasing forum, which is in effect a sub-group of the health authority, as GPs cannot legally hold a total budget on their own account outside fundholding. So for example, does the total purchasing group have the right unilaterally to purchase *in vitro* fertilization treatment if the host authority does not, or vice versa?

Developing a purchasing plan

The purchasing forum needs to develop a purchasing plan, which should take into account all national and regional priorities, as well as being co-ordinated with the health authority's local strategic plans. The deadline for publication of the 1996/7 purchasing plan was mid-September 1995 and would have to include any major shift notifications to providers. As well as notifying shifts between providers, this must include details of shifts of work into primary care, for example family planning to be moved from central clinics to general practice clinics or emergency admissions to be reduced by 5% by providing twilight nursing or a hospital-at-home scheme.

Essential reading for the total purchasing pilot will include the priorities and planning guidance for the NHS for the next year. As a subgroup of the health authority, the total purchasing group is obliged to (and of course should anyway) follow this guidance.

The guidance for 1996/7 can be summarized as follows.

Purpose of the NHS

The purpose of the NHS is to secure through the resources available the greatest possible improvement to the physical and mental health of the people of England by: promoting health, preventing ill-health, diagnosing and treating disease and injury, and caring for those with long-term illness and disability: a service available to all on the basis of clinical need, regardless of the ability to pay. In seeking to achieve this purpose the NHS, as a public service, aims to judge its performance under three headings – equity, efficiency and responsiveness.

How is this to be achieved?

The main government policies for achieving this are:

- the Health of the Nation strategy
- community care (Caring for People)
- the Patient's Charter
- a primary care-led NHS.

Implications for the total purchasing project

Fundholders are obliged to implement these policies anyway, so there should be no difficulties. A total purchasing pilot has a potential advantage in delivering a primary care-led NHS as GPs are steeped in the culture of primary care, whereas many health authorities are having to refocus their culture from secondary to primary care.

Baseline requirements and objectives

Purchasers are expected to meet the following standards:

- progress towards Health of the Nation targets

- Patient's Charter standards and guarantees
- waiting time targets and guarantees
- national and local efficiency targets
- agreed financial and activity targets
- control of drug expenditure
- sustained improvement in communications
- continued progress in the implementation of the National Information Management and Technology (IM&T) infrastructure.

Implications for the total purchasing project

The first four of these are requirements for fundholders, but the last four are likely to involve new disciplines or at least be considered by total purchasing pilots.

Agreed financial and activity targets

Total purchasing pilots will be expected to sign up to deliver efficiency gains within the efficiency index. This may present some theoretical difficulties as one of the purposes of total purchasing is to take work from secondary care (measured in the efficiency index) into primary care (not measured in the efficiency index). Thus a successful total purchasing pilot may appear inefficient according to standard efficiency index measurement. In practice this problem will probably not cause difficulties in the early years of total purchasing as fundholders will press for better counts in areas untouched by fundholding, for shorter waiting lists (increasing numbers treated in the transition years) and for more accurate counting of community activity. Moves to use more community hospitals may also increase activity.

   In financial terms the main objective for a total purchasing pilot will be not to overspend.

Control of drug expenditure

Control of drug expenditure has been one of the successes of fundholding, with slower rises in fundholding than in non-fundholding practices. At the present time drug budgets continue to be set and managed by health authorities, and overspends by an individual practice within a total purchasing pilot would be dealt with by the health authority rather than by the pilot.

Sustained improvement in communications

Total purchasing pilots are likely to be the subject of intense media scrutiny, particularly around the time of a general election. If they are successful this may worsen the two-tierism that fundholding itself has been said to create, and fundholders may be called to account for improving services faster than other GPs. To achieve success they will have to make choices between competing priorities, and may be challenged in the media about services from which they remove resources; for example removing resources from central family planning services to do the work in primary care to release resources for more community psychiatric nurses is more likely to be challenged by the media for the effects on the family planning service than for those on the mental health service. Total purchasing pilots need to consider public relations alongside their health authority and try to predict and prepare to defend controversial decisions.

Continued progress in the implementation of the IM&T infrastructure

This is likely to be an area of considerable interest to a total purchasing pilot, and an area to be considered will be better information links with hospitals and community services. It is hoped that all information within the NHS will eventually become as good as that of the Prescription Pricing Authority, which fundholders and health authorities rely on as the sole source of information on prescribing. Reliable contracting data will potentially cut transaction costs of endlessly cross-checking unreliable data.

Medium-term priorities

These are priorities that are to be worked towards over three to five years.

1 Work towards the development of a primary care-led NHS, in which decisions about the purchasing and provision of health care are taken as closely to patients as possible.

2 In partnership with local authorities to purchase and monitor a comprehensive range of secure, residential, inpatient and community services to enable patients with mental health illness to receive effective care and treatment in the most appropriate setting in accordance with their needs.

3 Improve the cost effectiveness of services throughout the NHS, and thereby secure the greatest health gain from the resources available, through formulating decisions on the basis of appropriate evidence about clinical effectiveness.

4 Give greater voice and influence to users of NHS services and their carers in their own care, the development and definition of standards set for NHS services locally and the development of NHS policies both locally and nationally.

5 Ensure in collaboration with local authorities and other organizations that integrated services are in place to meet needs for continuing health care and to allow elderly, disabled or vulnerable people to be supported in the community.

6 Develop NHS organizations as good employers with particular reference to work-force planning, education and training, employment policy and practice, the development of teamwork, reward systems, staff utilization and staff welfare.

Source: *The Priorities and Planning Guidance for the NHS* (1996/7)
EL (95) 68.

Implications for the total purchasing project

The delivery of the medium-term priorities will depend on the development of a more strategic approach by GPs. The partnership with the health authority will help as they bring considerable experience of strategic development to the partnership as well as the public health expertise necessary to deliver objective 3.

The implications of the medium-term priorities are considered in Table 5.1.

Local priorities

Total purchasing GPs will need to be fully aware of their health authority's strategic plans as they should generally be working within the same strategic framework, particularly where the plans have been drawn up with GP involvement. If the total purchasing group disagrees with any aspect of the plans, these will need to be discussed and resolved as plans will be difficult to implement without the full involvement of all purchasers.

An example of the importance of GP involvement is the planned closure of a large mental hospital. GPs need to be involved in this as they are dependent on the provision of good new services to ensure continuity and hopefully improvement of care to their patients, and may also need to contribute extra resources for lump costs of the transitional period of closure. The total purchasing pilot will need to identify from where to obtain the efficiency savings to fund its share of these closure costs.

Table 5.1: Implications of the medium-term priorities

Medium-term priority for NHS	Implication for total purchasing pilot
A Work towards the development of a primary care-led NHS, in which decisions about the purchasing and provision of health care are taken as close to patients as possible	As we have already observed GPs are extremely well placed to deliver a primary care-led NHS and are close to patients
B In partnership with local authorities, purchase and monitor a comprehensive range of secure, residential, inpatient and community services to enable patients with mental health illness to receive effective care and treatment in the most appropriate setting in accordance with their needs	Total purchasing pilots will need to work closely with their health authorities and social service departments to deliver this priority. In many areas of the country, mental health services have been historically under-resourced, and if total purchasers are as successful in identifying efficiency resources from the total purchasing budget as they have been from standard fundholding budgets, they may be able to bring extra resources to deliver priority B
C Improve the cost effectiveness of services throughout the NHS and thereby secure the greatest health gain from the resources available, through formulating decisions on the basis of appropriate evidence about clinical effectiveness	Total purchasing pilots are well placed to involve their GPs in the search for improved clinical effectiveness. Involvement with public health will be crucial in this. Purchasers are obliged to involve both provider clinicians and primary health care teams in strategies to secure sustained and comprehensive improvements in clinical effectiveness that demonstrate: • the use of evidence of clinical outcomes and the results of clinical audit to influence changes in services • their sources and use of information to judge the effectiveness of services or interventions • how patients are being informed about evidence of effectiveness related to their treatment. As an example of how well a total purchasing pilot is to implement priority C, there is now general recognition that too many grommets have been fitted without evidence of clinical effectiveness in preventing deafness. Reducing

Table 5.1: *continued*.

Medium-term priority for NHS	Implication for total purchasing pilot
C *continued*	the numbers inserted will depend on convincing GPs not to refer and not to raise parents' expectations on outcomes, and persuading ENT consultants to reduce the number of operations they perform. Success in implementing the policy can be audited. If it is to be effective the NHS will need to abandon old, ineffective treatments and rapidly adopt new, effective treatments, e.g. widespread and rapid adoption of early aspirin for acute myocardial infarcts, and better links between primary care and public health within total purchasing pilots should help
D Give greater voice and influence to users of NHS services and their carers in their own care, the development and definition of standards set for NHS services locally and the development of NHS policies, both locally and nationally	GPs are clearly ideally placed to involve individual patients in planning their own care, but it is much more difficult for GP purchasers to involve users of NHS services in the development of NHS policies. Many fundholders have performed patient surveys to inform their purchasing. In Berkshire we have CHC representation on the total purchasing project board and on the purchasing forum and plan to develop with them better ways of involving patients
E Ensure, in collaboration with local authorities and other organizations, that integrated services are in place to meet needs for continuing health care and to allow elderly, disabled or vulnerable people to be supported in the community	This will depend on the interaction between the social services department and the total purchasing pilot, which we describe more fully in Chapter 10. Again social service involvement on the project board should help to achieve this priority. Fundholding information systems are well placed to monitor readmission rates and inappropriate discharges
F Develop NHS organizations as good employers, with particular reference to work-force planning, education and training, employment policy and practice, the development of teamwork, reward systems, staff utilization and staff welfare	Developing NHS organizations as good employers is likely to be tackled in partnership with health authorities

Who should contract?

One of the strengths of fundholding has been the involvement of GPs and consultants in the contracting process. Total purchasing pilots will need to consider how to involve GPs and consultants in contracting without using too much of their clinical time. In Berkshire we have developed a system of contracting teams that negotiate directly with each clinical directorate. We usually have two or three GPs and two or three fund managers representing six total purchasing pilot practices and three associated fundholding practices in the fundholding consortium from which the total purchasing practices evolved. Negotiating directly with consultants is crucial as this ensures that agreements are feasible and will be delivered (as experience with fundholding taught us that where consultants were not involved, delivery often did not occur).

Developing pricing structures for total purchasing

It may well come as a surprise to new total purchasing GPs to discover that health authorities purchase care using an entirely different purchasing currency from that of GP fundholders. Fundholders have tended to purchase using banded prices, in which the price more or less equates to the cost, whereas many health authorities have tended to use average specialty cost, in which all procedures within a specialty are charged at the same price, or have tended to purchase an entire service on a block basis, where access to the service is given for a fixed price, for example a district family planning service for half a million pounds. Fundholders are likely to want to move to real prices as rapidly as possible as they will wish to pull resources out of hospitals as they bring work out into primary care. Sensitive pricing mechanisms will prove crucial to the success of a total purchasing pilot.

The first contracting task for the total purchasing pilot will be to determine the current price structures being used by their preferred providers, and to decide whether this structure will be sufficiently sensitive to allow the project to achieve its objectives. One option is for prices to be based on health care resource groups (HRGs), which are being developed by the National Casemix Office. Another option is to use prices that reflect the length of stay of individual patients. (HRG prices are based on length of stay as a proxy for cost but are not sensitive to the length of stay of individual patients.) These options are discussed below.

What are HRGs?

HRGs are clinically meaningful groups of treatments that are considered to use approximately the same level of resources. Groups are defined using primary and secondary procedures (OPCS 4 codes) and diagnoses (ICD 9 and 10 codes) and can be further split by age and complications or co-morbidities. There were in 1995 (Version 2) 528 groups divided into 16 chapters based on various body systems. HRGs are important to both purchasers and providers because they can be used to measure casemix within a contract.

How are HRGs developed?

HRGs are developed by panels of clinicians supported by the relevant college or association using information from minimum data sets and statistical advice from the National Casemix Office. They are subject to an ongoing refinement process to ensure that they keep pace with changes in medical practice.

Why use HRGs?

It has been compulsory in 1995/6 for every acute hospital to cost at least one specialty using HRGs and in 1996/7 to extend this to six specialties:

1 orthopaedics

2 ophthalmology

3 ENT

4 gynaecology

5 general surgery

6 urology.

Acute hospitals are also required to quote ECR prices on the basis of HRGs.

Further specialties will be added over subsequent years. Unfortunately HRGs do not coincide with fundholding price bands and discussions are underway to consider whether HRGs should be the contracting currency for fundholding, as it makes little sense for different purchasers to pay different prices for the same procedure and it should reduce transaction costs if all purchasers use the same purchasing currency. A letter issued by the purchasing branch of the NHS Executive (dated 4 December 1995) encourages providers to 'use the procedure costings underlying HRGs' as a basis for generating prices for fundholding. In North West region, groups of procedures for fundholding prices have been constructed out of HRGs.

HRGs are a vital contracting currency to total purchasers as they are likely to want to effect rapid change in casemix as they move work to primary care. Total purchasers may well take the less complex areas of care into primary care, leaving more complex treatments with the provider. Average specialty cost would be damaging to the provider, who would be delivering a more complex casemix at too low a price. Equally purchasers will want to keep an eye on a cash-strapped provider who changes the casemix to simpler procedures, collecting too high a price per procedure if using average specialty cost. It is in the interests of both parties to the contract to use HRGs. Some of the areas that total purchasers are more likely to want to influence are general medicine, elderly care and maternity, which are unfortunately the least developed HRG areas and, in the case of the first two, perhaps the most difficult to develop as there is such a wide-ranging casemix within the specialties. Further development work is being undertaken in these areas, particularly in elderly care. In the BIPP we have used HRGs for general medicine, gynaecology, orthopaedics and ophthalmology in the 1995/6 contracts and will extend their use to other specialties in future years.

Reducing lengths of stay

GPs will wish to ensure that resources accompany work into general practice, something that has often not happened as the NHS has moved to more day case surgery, earlier medical discharges and short hospital stays following delivery in obstetric units. Many of these pressures on primary care have not been accompanied by more community nurses and GPs. Many of the total purchasing pilots are using liaison nurses or occupational therapists to encourage earlier and better planned discharge, but there is no point in doing this if the pricing structure is based on average specialty cost as the price will be the same regardless of length of stay. A pricing structure incorporating lengths of stay is likely to be a high priority for a total purchaser. A contracting currency would ideally separate out medical costs from hotel costs, with high costs in the early stages of an acute hospital admission during maximal investigation or highest medical dependency and lower costs as the stay lengthened. Contracts based on days in hospital are relatively easy to develop for community hospitals or mental health hospitals as the cost is spread more evenly across the period of admission, but they are much more difficult to develop for acute medical services as costs may vary widely across the period of admission.

Experience of using more sensitive pricing

In Berkshire during our five live year, we have seen where we have made gains and losses through using more detailed price structures. For example in general medicine and general surgery we have experienced a reduced length of stay and lower cost casemix and have saved very significant sums compared with using average specialty prices that were based on a longer stay. However, in neonatal intensive care we have had several long episodes and have lost out compared to using average specialty prices. This latter example serves to demonstrate that there are risks inherent in this more sensitive approach, where payments to providers more accurately reflect their costs.

What types of contract should be used?

Many standard fundholders have been using cost per case contracts, but because changes in contracting intentions have to be notified six months in advance, the practices are effectively obliged to contract at the previous year's level unless they have notified providers in advance. Because the value of contracts is likely to be high particularly for larger population total purchasing pilots, cost and volume contracts are probably the most appropriate contracts to use for most pilots.

Are there areas of care that total purchasers should opt out of?

In general terms the more that is purchased through total purchasing, the nearer we can get to answering the question that has dogged fundholding from its inception. Is fundholding a more efficient way of developing health care than commissioning through health authorities, or is its success due to overfunding? This question is almost impossible to answer with conventional fundholding because of the difficulties of setting a fair budget for a restricted area of health care. However, if total purchasers opt out of areas of purchasing, the case will remain unproven.

There are inevitably some areas that cannot be purchased separately by a total purchasing pilot, for example genitourinary medicine, which is purchased on an anonymized patient basis, and health promotion, which is purchased across a district and the costs of which are not easily ascribed to an individual practice. In broad terms, however, we believe that total purchasing pilot GPs should purchase as much care as possible, but also pay some attention to risk management.

Small-volume external providers

By purchasing these with the health commission, the advantage of high-volume contract prices can be obtained, which are usually significantly less than ECR tariff costs. The health commission is informed of our anticipated volumes and casemix, which is added to theirs to produce a larger contract.

There are several advantages to this approach:

- reduced transaction costs for small-volume providers

- reduced transaction costs for the total purchasing pilot

- that it allows GPs to focus on local priorities with high-volume providers.

The total purchasing pilot is responsible for its own over- or underspends within the project.

Extracontractual referrals (ECRs)

Many health authorities have had difficulty controlling expenditure on ECRs. One of the great advantages of being a fundholding GP is the freedom to refer anywhere without going through elaborate procedures to obtain permission to refer outside a health authority contract. However, with this freedom has come responsibility and the recognition that resources spent at distant hospitals will have an impact on local services. The total purchasing pilot needs to decide how to handle ECR requests. In Berkshire we have set up a system of peer approval. Permission is sought from the GPs and the public health physician on the purchasing forum at the forum's regular meetings. For more urgent requests permission is sought from practice lead GPs by fax. Peer review works well, and we have often been able to point out to requesting GPs that there is an equally good service available locally. Involving GPs in ECR requests may also identify a service that should be but is not available locally, which can then be requested from a local Trust.

An advantage of peer review is that it takes away from individual GPs the decision to say no.

Risk management

The degree of risk that a total purchasing pilot exposes itself to depends on the size of the population. Even the largest pilots need to consider areas of risk and enter into risk sharing arrangements with their health authority. Some risks, such as the cost of bone marrow transplants and expensive blood products, are often covered by risk sharing arrangements between health authorities within a region. The total purchasing pilots need to identify and join these arrangements.

Forensic psychiatry can be highly expensive and is effectively controlled by the law courts rather than the NHS. In Berkshire we have agreed to pay a capitation share of all the county's forensic psychiatry costs, no matter whether all or none of the patients are ours.

Changing the pattern of health care

Total purchasers are likely to want to continue the process that they have achieved through fundholding, namely to provide appropriate care in primary care, ensure good access to secondary care and try to control rising emergency admission rates.

Priorities for change by GPs will depend on local services but will usually include medical and elderly care emergencies, A&E unit usage, maternity care, family planning and mental health provision.

Controlling emergency admissions

Emergency admissions have been rising steadily over several years, although the precise level of increase has been difficult to measure because of difficulties in data collection in Trusts. Areas of confusion include:

- FCE (finished consultant episodes) inflation (one admission may trigger several FCEs if several different consultants see the patient)

- shorter lengths of stay for elective and emergency admissions, which may cause more readmissions.

There are a number of possible stratagems for fundholders to control emergency admissions, including:

- the purchase of more community beds, although proper pricing is necessary to be sure that these really are more cost effective than acute sector beds. Nursing home beds are an alternative where there is no local community hospital

- devolving nursing budgets into practices to allow practices to look after patients at home, by either using agency nurses at night or developing twilight visiting services with community Trusts

- developing hospital-at-home schemes.

In seeking to reduce emergency admissions, total purchasers will need to be reassured that they are not merely substituting their own time and work-load as a free good to replace expensive emergency admissions.

As well as influencing numbers of admissions, total purchasing groups will wish to influence lengths of stay, perhaps by using liaison nurses, practice based occupational therapists and elderly care health visitors to work closely with local hospitals and social service departments to ensure that bed blocking does not occur due to lack of community facilities.

A&E departments

Many total purchasing GPs have been amazed at the large-scale inappropriate use of A&E departments uncovered by the need for Trusts to provide clinical information in order to be paid for activity. Redirecting this inappropriate attendance to primary care would not necessarily reduce costs as staffing commitments to cover major trauma incidents would need to be maintained. There is considerable scope for reducing inappropriate A&E attendance by providing better access to triage nurses in primary care, although resources would need to come out of the A&E department to fund such posts. The problem of extra work for busy GPs without payment will need to be addressed before all GPs will enthusiastically embrace a move of minor A&E work to primary care.

A beneficial spin-off of redirection of A&E work to primary care might well be a reduction in emergency admissions as GPs are more likely to keep patients out of hospital than are recently qualified senior house officers.

Maternity services

Total purchasers will need to consider the Changing Childbirth reports in contracting for maternity services. These reports were issued by the Expert Maternity Group in 1993 (Part I: Report of the Expert Maternity Group; Part II: Survey of Good Communication Practice in Maternity Services). Changing Childbirth is essentially about recognizing pregnancy as a natural process rather than a medical process and allowing women to be at the centre of decisions about their own care.

In order to understand the scale of the task in implementing Changing Childbirth, it is worth listing the indicators of success identified by the Changing Childbirth team. Within five years:

1 all women should be entitled to carry their own notes

2 every woman should know one midwife who ensures continuity of care – the named midwife

3 at least 30% of women should have the midwife as the lead professional

4 every woman should know the lead professional who has a key role in the planning and provision of her care

5 at least 75% of women should know the person who cares for them during their delivery

6 midwives should have direct access to some beds in all maternity units

7 at least 30% of women delivered in a maternity unit should be admitted under the management of a midwife

8 the total number of antenatal visits for women with uncomplicated pregnancies should have been reviewed in the light of the available evidence and the Royal College of Obstetrics and Gynaecology (RCOG) guidelines

9 all front-line ambulances should have a paramedic able to support the midwife who needs to transfer a woman to hospital in an emergency

10 all women should have access to information about the services available in their locality.

Source: (1993) *Changing Childbirth* Part I Report of the Expert Maternity Group. HMSO, London.

This presents a fairly daunting agenda for change, and total purchasers will need to work closely with health authorities, maternity units, obstetricians and midwives to deliver these changes. Very limited resources have been made available nationally to deliver Changing Childbirth, so fund-holders' experience of identifying efficiency savings to improve other community services, such as community nursing, physiotherapy and coun-selling, will be crucial in delivering Changing Childbirth.

Family planning

Family planning services have developed through two principal routes:

1 a community based service often developed by the Family Planning Association, originally and subsequently taken over by health author-ities and later individual Trusts

2 a service in primary care.

Some areas have rationalized their community clinics as comprehensive general practice clinics have developed, but in some areas two parallel services exist, with patients free to attend either. Total purchasing GPs providing a comprehensive family planning service may wish to ration-alize their purchasing of a parallel community service, perhaps encour-aging clinics to develop services for teenagers and specialist referrals, while cutting back on general services. This will need close liaison with the community health council, and practices may need to consider the pro-vision of evening sessions to replace lost community clinics. Clear explan-ation of where efficiency savings will be reinvested will help put the case across as there is a widespread belief that patients should have a choice of family planning service. Reinvesting savings in an inaccessible secondary care service, for example shortening a neurology clinic waiting list by providing resources for an extra consultant, will strengthen the case as patients with long waits for neurology services do not have much choice. One good service for family planning and one for neurology may be better than two good family planning services and a poor neurology service.

Mental health

Fundholders have had limited impact on mental health services as inpatient care has been excluded from budgets. Change has focused on services for the less severely mentally ill, with services such as psychology counselling, psychiatric consultant outpatient referrals and community psychiatric nurse referrals all purchased by fundholders and frequently brought into primary care outreach clinics. Total purchasing, which also covers inpatient services, will increase GPs' involvement in purchasing services for the more severely mentally ill and will require close collaboration with other agencies, notably mental health Trusts, social services and voluntary agencies.

The care programme approach (CPA)

The movement of severely mentally ill patients from old-style psychiatric hospitals to the community results in a complex interlinking of services involving multiple agencies. The CPA has the following components:

- a detailed needs assessment

- a comprehensive care plan

- care monitored and reviewed on a regular basis

- involvement of patients and carers in the process.

The CPA was introduced in 1991 and requires DHAs and local authority social service departments to put in place specified arrangements for the care and treatment of mentally ill people in the community. The CPA has four main components:

1 systematic arrangements for assessing the health and social needs of people accepted by the specialist psychiatric services

2 the formulation of a care plan that addresses the identified health and social care needs

3 the appointment of a key worker to keep in close touch with the patient and monitor care

4 regular review and, if need be, agreed changes to the care plan.

The CPA is an approach rather than a precise prescription, and negotiations involving GPs should be carried out at local level.

Supervised discharge (after care under supervision)

The Mental Health (Patients in the Community) Bill introduces supervised discharge for certain patients detained under the Mental Health Act 1983. It includes the introduction of supervision registers. Supervised discharge is designed for 'revolving door' patients who go through repeated cycles of admission under the Mental Health Act, followed by breakdown of arrangements for care in the community, often because they stop medication or lose contact with aftercare services. A patient subject to supervised discharge will be required to abide by the terms of the care plan and will be supervised, usually by the key worker, who has powers to require the patient to reside in a specified place and attend for medical treatment and rehabilitation, and convey a patient to a place where he or she is to attend for treatment.

Fundholders are obliged to contract for the CPA approach, and additional guidance suggests that they should also stipulate that:

- the patient's GP is always invited to care planning meetings

- the practice receives copies of aftercare plans within five days

- the key worker should be in regular contact with the practice.

Supervision registers

Supervision registers were introduced from April 1994 to identify people with a severe mental illness who may be a significant risk to themselves or others, and to ensure that local services focus effectively on these patients, who have the greatest need for care and active follow-up. Provider units are responsible locally for supervision registers.

Consideration for inclusion on the register should take place as part of the care programme, either initially or at review. Patients with a severe mental illness should be included if they are at significant risk of committing serious violence, of suicide or of severe self-neglect. The patient should be informed that he or she is on the register. The supervision register is effectively a sub-section of the CPA.

Total purchasers as a sub-group of the health authority need to be involved in the development of local mental health services and will need to stipulate in their contracts adherence to the CPA and supervision registers.

Cancer services

Cancer services are not part of standard fundholding, and total purchasing pilots will need to work closely with health authorities both to meet Health of the Nation standards on cancer and to develop appropriate and effective services, taking into account 'A Policy Framework for Commissioning Cancer Services – a Report by the Expert Advisory Group on Cancer to the Chief Medical Officers of England and Wales', which proposes profound changes to the way in which cancer services are delivered. This report recommends that all patients should have access to a uniformly high quality of care in the community or hospital, wherever they may live, to ensure the maximum possible cure rates and best quality of life. Care should be provided as close to the patient's home as is compatible with high-quality, safe and effective treatment. To achieve this the report recommends that cancer care should be built on a network extending from primary care through cancer units in district hospitals to cancer centres. The three levels of care proposed are:

1 *primary care* – detailed discussions will be needed between primary care teams, units and centres to clarify referral and follow-up protocols

2 designated *cancer units* in district hospitals of a size to support clinical teams with sufficient expertise to manage the more common cancers. These will not normally provide radiotherapy unless geographically isolated

3 designated *cancer centres* providing expertise in the management of all cancers, including common cancers in their immediate locality and less common cancers referred from cancer units. They will provide radiotherapy.

The cancer unit will need to be of sufficient size to allow surgical (and medical) sub-specialization in reasonable volumes of work in each of the common cancers. Less common cancers should be treated at cancer centres. The cancer unit will need to work closely with the cancer centre, and oncologists should normally work in both.

The cancer centre should function as a cancer unit for its local population as well as providing treatment for less common cancers. Surgeons and physicians with special skills should practise here. They should serve a population of at least two thirds of a million (optimally a million) and provide services for children and adolescents with cancer.

Both cancer units and centres should develop close links with primary care and treat patients in partnership with primary care teams. Good communication is vital.

In order to contribute to these profound changes, total purchasers will need to work closely with their local health authority as well as other health authorities. Changes will be difficult as local radiotherapy services not designated as cancer centres will have to close and GPs will want to ensure that a sensible compromise is reached between loss of local services and provision of specialist expertise in more distant cancer centres, requiring sick patients to travel.

Consulting the public

When contracting for change it is vital to be aware of the requirement to consult the public. Guidance on consultation is given in an NHS Executive circular 'Consultation and Involving the Consumer'.

Before deciding on any change it is prudent to have discussions with the community health council (CHC) and any special interest groups. Once prospective change has been formalized into a plan, it may then need to be formally presented to the CHC. This is required for:

- a major closure

- a substantial development

- a substantial variation of the service.

Rights of CHCs

CHCs have a right to:

- relevant information from local NHS authorities

- access to certain NHS properties

- be consulted on substantial developments or variations in service

- meetings with matching NHS authorities.

Definition of consultation

The essence of consultation is the communication of a genuine invitation to give advice and a genuine receipt of that advice.

Content of consultation

- It is for the authority to determine the form, content, extent and timing of consultation.

- The principle should be to ensure a full degree of interested parties, including consumers at all stages of strategic and operational change.

Involving the public

Much importance is attached to engaging the public in purchasing decisions. This is no easy task. To make a contribution the public have to be informed on the desirability of a service change, the effectiveness of that change, and its cost and likely impact on other services.

Bromley Health Authority has carried out some outstanding work in that field by holding meetings with people of different age groups and social class. Any purchaser would be well advised to obtain their report.

Contracting areas less likely to be subject to early change by total purchasers

We have identified above some of the areas likely to be of interest to and subject to change by a total purchasing pilot, but clearly a total purchaser is responsible for purchasing a comprehensive service and the following areas will also need consideration.

NHS breast screening services

Practices tend to be called in on a three-yearly cycle. However, it would seem more sensible for a total purchasing pilot to purchase an annual capitation share of the whole health authority's service rather than cost per case contracts when its patients are screened.

Dentistry

The NHS Executive has issued guidelines to total purchasing pilots for funding arrangements to take account of the proportion of the project's patients treated by hospital and community dental services. If a project wished to set separate contracts, it should agree this both with local representatives of the dental profession and the health authority.

We have not attempted to produce a comprehensive list of all the services that are purchased by a total purchaser, who by definition purchases everything, but have focused on areas most likely to be subject to change by GPs. At least initially, services not discussed are likely to be purchased in the same way as by the total purchasing pilot's host health authority.

6

The individual fund manager's role
Janet Fitzgerald

Resource implications

Taking on the responsibility for a total fund inevitably has resource implications; these can be examined under separate headings, as discussed below.

Staff

There will inevitably be an increased administrative and managerial workload. The nature and extent of this increase will vary depending on the structure of the project. If a practice is going single handed into total purchasing, it will need to assess its current staff structure, examine the anticipated requirements for total purchasing and plan accordingly. If the practice is to be part of a 'multifund', a number of additional issues will need to be considered.

- Is there to be a project manager?
- Is there to be some element of central administration?
- If so, how much?
- What will the reporting structure be?
- What will be the source and mechanism for funding?

The approach to data collection and validation in the preparatory year will also need to be considered.

- Will the practice/multifund be collecting and validating a whole financial year's data or a set number of months?
- Are all types of activity going to be counted and validated to the same extent?

• Will the existing computer system be used? If not will data need to be keyed twice or will there be an electronic data interchange?

The answers to all the above questions will have a significant effect on the resourcing requirements for an individual practice.

Having established the project structure and quantified the data and administration requirements, a practice will need to look closely at its existing resources. Should a practice use existing staff or employ an incremental team member? There are advantages and disadvantages to both scenarios. The existing team, if their hours can be increased, are already familiar with fundholding, medical terminology and personnel at both provider units and the health authority; however, consideration would have to be given to the timing of workload as standard fundholding deadlines and timetables are likely to be broadly similar to those of total purchasing, leading to bottlenecks of work. Where expansion of the existing team is not possible, or the size of the practice and therefore the workload requires more input than could be provided by current staffing levels, a new member of staff will need to be recruited; this brings a different set of issues to consider. As total purchasing is still in its experimental stages, with practices involved in pilot projects either as single funds or as part of consortia for a specified period (usually one preparatory year and perhaps one live year), any new members of staff should be employed under a fixed-term contract to minimize any ongoing financial risk to the practice. The job description should be carefully constructed, listing specific responsibilities relating to total purchasing (Box 6.1). Are the responsibilities to be covered by the fundholding team during any absence for holidays, training or sickness? Will the new staff member be expected to provide reciprocal cover for standard fundholding?

When planning for the introduction of total purchasing, consult with existing team members, get their input on how they see the project working from an administrative point of view, involve them in recruitment and keep them informed of the project's progress. Just as in standard fundholding, good communication and teamwork are the keys to success.

Staff training

The whole practice needs to be informed of the decision to begin total purchasing and the rationale behind it. This is essential if the project is to be successful. Clinical members of the team need to understand the significance of their clinical practice in relation to the fund, for example the decision to admit a patient versus providing care in the home, or policies

Box 6.1: Sample job description

Job title:	Administration assistant
Accountable to:	Fundholding manager
Hours:	By agreement
Duties:	Assist with the day-to-day running of the total purchasing computer system, including daily back-up procedures, fault logging and liaison with the central fundholding office concerning data transfer and month end closure.
	Sorting, photocopying and distribution of clinical mail.
	Validating patient activity data received from providers and subsequent data entry on the total purchasing system according to set protocols. Reporting of errors and omissions to the provider units involved and escalation of unsolved items to the fund manager/ central office.
	Assisting with the set-up of the system at the start of each financial year.
	Assisting with monitoring returns required by the central office.
	Assisting with quality monitoring as required.
	Checking and processing of hospital invoices, including handling of queries and correspondence with providers.
	Validation and progress chasing of patients waiting for elective hospital procedures.
	Maintaining accurate and complete data files.
	Attending appropriate meetings and training sessions.
	Providing departmental relief cover (fundholding and non-fundholding).
	Such other duties as are agreed with the partnership.

on ECRs (are there any restricted services or services that the practice does not intend to purchase at all?).

The fundholding administration team needs further training on the protocols established for recording of clinical and contractual data (it being preferable that they are if at all possible involved in the setting of the protocols), the computer system to be used and the document flows, both within the practice and between the practice and providers or any central administration office.

If the practice is working with other practices for the purpose of total purchasing, it is extremely beneficial if training sessions can be run on a joint basis rather than in individual practices; this encourages cross-fertilization of ideas and avoids reinventing the wheel!

Other costs

These include those for stationery, telephone, faxes, photocopying and other consumables involved in the expanded administration activities. If a new staff member is recruited, he or she will need a work-station (desk, chair, computer and telephone).

It is essential that the funding mechanisms for all the above resources are agreed before the practice enters into any financial commitments.

Fund manager's role

Management input to the process is another important factor not to be overlooked; this will consist of planning, budgeting, contracting, monitoring and reporting; in other words more of the same activities as are involved in good standard fund management. It will either be necessary to delegate some existing responsibilities or to increase the number of management hours available in order to manage total purchasing. There is also an inevitable increase in the number of meetings that require a practice presence; it helps if the burden of representation can be shared with the lead GP.

The role of the individual fund manager will vary according to the size and structure of the total purchasing project. In a single practice project, staff supervision, liaison or negotiation with provider units, activity and cost monitoring and management of the computer system will all require additional input relating to the 'total' element of the fund. In addition there will be extra work involved in ensuring (with the help of the lead GP) that all members of the primary health care team are aware of the implications of total purchasing and are kept up to date with any changes in patient services that come about as a result of the project, for example a change of provider or new services. The fund manager will also be involved in budget negotiations and contract negotiations for the project; this can be particularly time-consuming at a time when the standard fundholding workload is also heavy. On an ongoing basis **two** month ends and **two** year ends will need to be managed and completed successfully.

Where the practice is part of a 'multifund', some of the management tasks can be shared between all the fund managers in the project, and if there is a project manager he or she will shoulder some of the burden. The following are some of the areas that could be shared:

- contract negotiation
- budget negotiation
- data validation
- contract monitoring
- attendance at meetings.

If agreement can be reached on scope and authority, sub-groups of managers could assume responsibilities for certain specialties or hospitals on behalf of the whole project, thus reducing the amount of individual input required at a practice level. Just as in the general staffing issues, the reporting structure and responsibilities of individual managers and the 'central office' should be agreed and documented during the preparatory phase of the project to ensure that effective fund management is established.

One of the key roles of the fund manager during the project will be to present information to the practice both to inform and to facilitate planned changes. In a single practice project, the reporting capabilities of the computer system will need to be examined and a range of management information reports constructed to provide the necessary information on a timely basis. Where a 'central office' exists it will need to be established where management information is to be produced, in what format and to what timescales, and whether practices will share individual practice or GP data or whether consolidated reports will be produced.

Information handling

Just as was required for standard fundholding, the data flow within the practice should be reviewed. All clinical data must be passed through the fundholding team for sorting and processing. It should be a specific individual's responsibility to photocopy the mail (ensuring no delay in the original document being seen by the relevant GP and filed in the clinical notes) and sort it into fundholding and non-fundholding categories. Fundholding mail will be processed as normal, and the non-fundholding mail will be validated and processed according to agreed protocols. Protocols for handling non-fundholding data will need to be agreed during the preparatory year. MDSs and waiting lists will need to be received for non-fundholding activity in order for validation to take place. Validation takes the form of cross-checking clinical data with hospital data and vice versa to identify errors and omissions, which should then be reported back to the provider units for correction. Validated activity is then processed on the computer system.

The following are some of the categories of activity that will require systems or protocols in place for processing.

- *Non-fundholding elective procedures (in and day cases)* – From 1996/7 the list of services and procedures covered by standard fundholding will be increased significantly, leaving the number of non-fundholding elective procedures for any one practice likely to be very small. These will, however, be expensive procedures and therefore require careful recording and monitoring.

- *Non-fundholding outpatients* – All outpatient attendances at clinics not covered by the fundholding scheme must be accounted for.

- *Emergency admissions (acute and psychiatric)* – This is a key additional area for total purchasing, and the data recording requirements must be carefully considered. The activity will need to be recorded to allow accurate pricing of the episode in accordance with the contract terms, for example specialty banding, OPCS code, HRG code, number of bed days, etc.

- *A&E* – This area of activity is one in which there has traditionally been incomplete information of a clinical and contractual nature. During the preparatory year systems will need to be developed with provider A&E departments to ensure that all relevant patient activity is notified to the GP. A methodology will need to be established to handle the small percentage of A&E attendances in which the patient's GP is not identified.

- *Patient transport (ambulance)* – Similar to A&E a method of recording patient transport activity will need to be established. Ambulance activity falls into one of three categories: 'blue-light' emergencies, 'doctor's urgent' and patient transport (pre-booked hospital attendances). The recording of the activity will depend largely on the type of contract negotiated.

This is not an exhaustive list; a full list of all areas of patient activity outside the scope of standard fundholding should be drawn up during the preparatory year, and a method for recording each category must be devised. However, just as in the preparation for standard fundholding, it may not be possible for every item of patient activity to be validated in the early stages of total purchasing; priority will need to be given to those areas that feature prominently in the purchasing plan for the live project year.

In conclusion the key elements for effective total fund management are the same as for standard fundholding:

- good communication within the practice, within any multifund and between all other parties to the project, including patients, providers and the health authority

- good GP involvement

- clearly defined organizational structures and responsibilities

- the appropriate quality and quantity of staff adequately trained and informed

- effective administration systems.

7

Information management

Fran Butler

Brian Mawhinney, when Minister for Health, described information as the life-blood of a purchasing organization. It is required in practical terms for contract monitoring and in more strategic terms for assessing the needs of the population and planning services. For a total purchasing project, as for fundholding and health authority purchasing, good information is fundamental, as is the ability to manage it well and make use of it to support purchasing decisions. In many ways good information has underpinned the Berkshire project's successes, and information shortfalls have been the source of some of its greatest frustrations.

This chapter discusses some of the information requirements, outlines the information related tasks for the preparatory year, and describes the information system needs. It also describes how information is being used to support decision making and paints a vision of the future in which information handling is streamlined and transaction costs much reduced.

Information is required for several key purposes, chiefly:

- contract management (including monitoring)
- needs assessment and service planning
- to support GP decision making.

Information requirements are described under the first two headings, and the third, supporting decision making, is covered towards the end of this chapter.

Information requirements for contract management

Information requirements should always flow from 'business' objectives (see Chapter 4). Information collected has a cost, and in the health care market additional costs incurred by the provider in collecting information will inevitably be passed on to purchasers. It is therefore important to agree with providers an appropriate level of information detail required to support each service to be purchased, and to ensure that the information provides sufficient benefit to justify its cost of collection.

Total purchasing projects are venturing into purchasing terrain previously covered only by authorities. Information coverage of these services will have been driven by the purchasing aspirations and information needs of authorities rather than of GP purchasers. Health authorities are likely to be receiving patient based information for inpatient and consultant outpatient work, but probably little else. Services such as family planning and A&E are likely to be supported by aggregate figures only, based on manual data collection methods.

By contrast, these less-scrutinized areas may be among those which GPs wish to purchase on a cost per case or cost and volume basis, with a view to making the service more appropriate to the needs of patients and eliminating potential waste and duplication of services provided more cost effectively in primary care. In order for a total purchasing project to have its own separate schedule for a service, the provider must be able to produce service utilization figures split between the total purchasing practices and other residents for which the health authority is responsible.

Successes

The following examples show how the provision of data has allowed BIPP to develop its own contract rather than sharing the health authority's.

- A&E – As a result of BIPP the Royal Berkshire Hospital is now producing good quality A&E data for practices, and GPs are able to assess the appropriateness of the service being supplied (as well as receiving better clinical data about their patients). It is therefore now possible for us to have our own contract for purchase of A&E services on a cost and volume basis. A significant amount of inappropriate usage of the service has been identified as a result, and the project must now decide what use to make of this knowledge.

- West Berkshire Priority Care Services Trust has been able to supply us with patient specific data in a number of areas in which this had not been available before (e.g. contacts for specialist nurse services such as diabetic and breast care); the only services purchased on a block basis from this Trust are those which cannot be separated out by practice (e.g. health promotion).

- The Royal Berkshire Ambulance Trust has been able to supply data about the number of 'GP urgent' calls, and we are embarking on a separate contract for these.

Frustrations

GP aspirations of purchasing all services on a project specific basis may have to be tempered by the realities of information availability. Areas in which GPs wished to purchase on a cost and volume basis but were unable to because of lack of information include the following.

- *Family planning* – initially no patient specific data sets were available, and the lack of these detailed data from the beginning of the year initially prevented us from setting our own contract for the service. A system was then introduced, and (subject to patient confidentiality protocols) practices will shortly be receiving MDSs allowing us to check whether or not the aggregate data we have been given are accurate. A cost per case contract is shortly due to be in operation for family planning.

- *Mental health* – although we were able to identify and purchase mental health inpatient care separately from the health authority, data are not as yet available electronically, meaning that it is very difficult to perform systematic analyses to determine the nature of usage within this service.

There have been considerable difficulties with the aggregate data provided by Trusts to support contract monitoring because of changing definitions, particularly the acute Trust's definition of emergencies. This has made it difficult for the project to determine whether or not it is achieving its objective of coping with the rise in emergencies. Advice from Berkshire would be to ensure that all parties are working to the same definitions (e.g. of whether 'emergencies' includes sick babies born in hospital or not) and to have these documented in the contract.

Information requirements will change from year to year and will become more demanding as GP purchasing becomes more comprehensive and provider information capabilities grow. It is important to remember:

- not to agree contracts that cannot practically be monitored

- that information availability is likely initially to restrict purchasing ambitions in some areas.

Contract monitoring should also include performance against Patient's Charter targets. In Berkshire this has so far been left to the health authority, except for monitoring of waiting times, but other projects might wish to receive their own Patient's Charter monitoring data.

Information for needs assessment and planning services

Five years on from the inception of the internal market, it is true to say that in some areas purchasers are simply purchasing what the provider is providing, i.e. the service that is purchased is being defined by the provider. GPs have day-to-day contact with users of services and in many ways are in a better position than health authorities to challenge sacred cows and to provide a catalyst for rationalizing services that may not be effective, changing contracts to reflect this. Good information is needed to be able to assess the health care needs of the project's population (i.e. the patients of the participating practices) and to plan to purchase services to address those needs.

Practices already have, stored in their clinical systems, a wealth of information about their registered population. The intuitive knowledge of GPs and the primary health care team as a whole is also an important resource for assessing needs. Other information that can be made available to support purchasing includes prescribing data and census variables for the project catchment area. The total purchasing scheme will also require data for monitoring Health of the Nation targets for the project population. In terms of support for GPs in making evidence based decisions, the Cochrane Database is being expanded into an important tool. Public health departments can also advise or point GPs towards useful documents.

Data collection and validation in the preparatory year

As described in Chapter 4, a key objective for the preparatory year is to collect and validate information about usage of services by the project's population, in order to enable contracts to be set on a sound basis and to ensure that the project is on a good financial footing (i.e. that one can predict expenditure with reasonable accuracy before the year commences).

Data collection by the provider should commence in April of the preparatory year for those areas in which data are not already available but which have been highlighted by the GPs as being of high priority. As soon as possible after the end of a month, patient specific data should be forwarded to practices and aggregate data (for shadow contract monitoring) made available both at practice and project levels. Practices can then validate the data and let the provider know of any discrepancies, which can then be corrected. Experience in Berkshire was that data were of reasonably good quality from both our main providers (although data quality for inpatients was better than that for outpatients), so the detailed data validation exercise was carried out for six months' data only. Problems with the data included:

- data sets being included for patients not registered with the practice

- no clinical evidence (e.g. no discharge letter)

- some data items not matching the data available at the practice (e.g. the procedure wrongly coded)

- discharge letters being received by the practice where no data set was received.

Such problems were similar to those experienced with fundholding data.

Data validation by practices in the preparatory year allows the project to measure the quality of the data to be used for contract setting for the live year. If data quality is good, practices and providers will have confidence in using the data for contract setting. If data quality is poor, the project will need to work with the provider to improve on the data before they can be used for contract setting. Poor data, or data whose quality is unknown, represent a risk to both purchaser and provider in a new contracting environment such as that offered by total purchasing.

Information systems

The support of an information system will be required for monitoring contracts. It is essential that sufficient time and thought is given to defining the requirements for such a system. The following questions will need to be debated between practices, the authority and providers.

- How will contracts be monitored? Which organization (practices or health authority) will:
  - record commitments
  - validate MDSs and how much effort is available in practices

- record MDSs on the system (or input data sets to the system)
- validate invoices
- keep a record of invoices received and paid?

- Are providers willing to send data directly to practices, or will the authority separate data for the participating practices from the data relating to all its residents?

- For which services do data sets need to be held at patient level?

- How detailed are the prices – can financial monitoring easily be calculated from aggregate data?

- Are practices funded to perform detailed data validation and data entry onto a fundholding type system?

- How much funding is available for purchase and subsequent support of information technology equipment?

- To what extent is the system required to be a tool for needs assessment and planning services as well as contract monitoring?

Once the configuration for data and information management is reasonably well defined, it is time to look at the possible options available to support contract management and to assess how well these fit requirements. Three possible options are given below.

- *Implement a modified fundholding system* – a fundholding system modified to accept non-fundholding data, and also modified in other minor ways, could be implemented. Either a separate system can be purchased or participating practices could implement the 'total purchasing add-on' from the supplier of their fundholding system. Several suppliers offer total purchasing add-ons, which is an attractive option for single practice schemes, but it is important to determine what the system actually does and whether this meets the project needs.

- *Provide access to the health authority's system* – most (if not all) health authorities run systems that contain contracting data sets for inpatient (and outpatient) activity for their residents. With this option a total purchasing scheme could access the data for the participating practices from within this system.

- *Develop a custom-built spreadsheet or database* – a project may decide that it wants its own monitoring database but does not need much of the functionality of a fundholding system. A simple database can be set up to hold all of the contract data sets for the project, in a way that can be analysed for contract monitoring and purchasing decision support. Data sets could be loaded up electronically, with invalid data sets being deleted manually following validation.

Table 7.1 summarizes the advantages and disadvantages of each of these options.

If little effort for validation and data input is available in practices, a total purchasing scheme would need to choose between using a modified fundholding system with high levels of automated validation and input, or 'piggy-backing' on a health authority system, accepting that not all areas have detailed data and that it may not be possible to record commitments. It is useful to note that there is as yet no requirement on total purchasing schemes to account for expenditure in as detailed a manner as for fund-holding, and therefore no requirement to use a fundholding type system.

In Berkshire a modified fundholding system was chosen to support con-tract management, after tenders had been sought from several suppliers. Use of the health authority's system was considered but the idea rejected for the following reasons.

- Recording of commitments was not possible.

- The system only catered for inpatient and outpatient MDSs.

- The option for practices to view their own data (and not data from any other practice) was not available.

- The system was not in a sufficiently advanced state of implementation at the health authority for its use to be extended to practices.

The following modifications were required to make the fundholding system chosen suitable for use within a total purchasing scheme:

- accounting on the basis of episode end date (as at 1995/6 fundholding uses episode start date to define the accounting month; health authority purchasing uses the end date, and we needed to be able to conform to this for reporting purposes)

- additional treatment codes were required in order to be able to enter non-fundholding activity (e.g. for mental health inpatients, obstetrics, renal dialysis, wheelchairs, etc.).

Each practice has its own copy of the system and downloads its data on a regular basis to the central BIPP office. This configuration (Figure 7.1) allows practices to monitor their own performance against contracts,

Table 7.1: Assessment of possible options for a contract management system

Option	Advantages	Disadvantages
Modified fundholding system	• Accepts a generic data set, allowing data for any service to be collected	• System may not hold the full MDS, limiting use for data analysis (diagnosis field is particularly important for analysis of emergencies and may not be catered for)
	• Contracts can be set up, including price, allowing almost any complexity of price structure to be monitored	• Data input is labour intensive unless facilities exist for electronic transfer
	• Monitors financial position of contracts	• In a multipractice project it may not be possible to integrate with existing clinical or fundholding systems
	• Practices familiar with system and available reports	• May be an expensive solution and provide functionality that is not required (bearing in mind that audit at the fundholding level of detail does not yet apply to total purchasing)
	• Caters for commitment accounting (but limited need for this – very little elective work)	• Setting up contracts is time-consuming if there are a large number of price bands
	• In single practice projects it may be possible to extend the fundholding system to total purchasing with little capital cost or training, maintaining links with the clinical system	• Comparative analysis against data for the rest of the authority population is not possible
	• Ownership of data management process by practices	• Too expensive (in terms of information technology and clerical input) for roll-out to all practices; therefore not a strategic solution for locality/GP-led purchasing across the health authority population

Table 7.1: *continued.*

Option	Advantages	Disadvantages
Access to health authority system	• Potentially cheap and strategic option • Enables comparative analysis between total purchasing scheme data and health authority-wide data • No additional data input required • Additional data to support needs assessment and planning may be available (e.g. public health data sets, census data, etc.) • Complete MDS held	• Modifications required for data confidentiality; practice staff must not be able to view data relating to another practice • Most health authority systems do not contain practice registers – comparison against the clinical system is still required for validation purposes • Most health authority systems do not cater for input of generic MDSs • Possible problems if ownership perceived to rest with the health authority • Commitment accounting may not be available
Simple custom-built database or spreadsheet	• Cheap • Total control of design and ongoing development rests with project • Potentially short lead time • Full practice ownership of data management • Allows for input of MDSs from providers in electronic form without double keying (if this is done it needs a mechanism to allow invalid data to be deleted)	• Unlikely to interface with other systems • Limited functionality (but may be adequate)

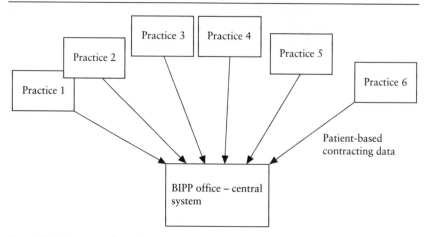

Figure 7.1: System configuration.

without being able to view data from any other practice. It also allows the BIPP office to monitor progress against contracts as a whole and expenditure across all practices.

Experience in Berkshire has shown that system implementation across this number of practices is not a trivial task, and the system does not provide all of the functionality required. Particular problems encountered have been:

- the complexity of the HRG and length of stay based prices, meaning that registering contracts on the system was several days work and practice staff needed considerable hand-holding in selection of the correct treatment

- that the implementation effort required has impacted severely on the effort available for data analysis to support GPs in changing services.

Many total purchasing schemes are using, or planning to use, modified fundholding systems to manage contracts, while others are taking the approach that their own practice view of the health authority's system, or the use of tailored spreadsheets or a simple database, offers them adequate facilities for this purpose as well as other advantages. At the time of writing the Berkshire project is considering use of the modified fundholding system: in 1996/7 there is little elective work in fundholding and so the need to be able to record commitments and track referrals largely disappears.

Information analysis to support GP decision making

Information collected by the project is available not only for contract management but also to support GPs in their efforts to change the way in which services are provided and used, and to measure whether project objectives are being achieved.

One of the major objectives of the Berkshire project was to cope with the rise in emergency admissions, with a view to explaining and stemming this rise. Data analyses so far shown to GPs have included:

- percentages of emergency admissions referred by GP (Figure 7.2)

- bar charts of numbers of referrals per GP for each practice

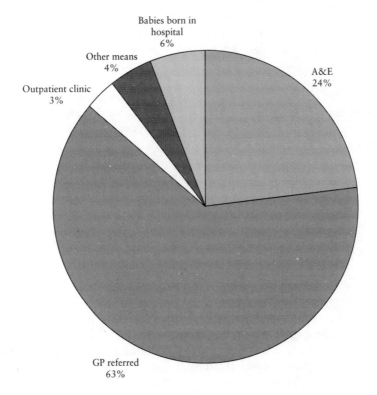

Figure 7.2: BIPP emergency admissions to Royal Berkshire and Battle Hospitals NHS Trust, April–October 1995.

- list of top ten diagnoses for each practice and for the project overall (see Table 7.2), which demonstrates to GPs in a practice how their admissions may be differing from those of the project overall, and where to concentrate their efforts to reduce emergencies

- analysis of the ways in which the number of emergency admissions varies from month to month, and whether this is different between the project population and the Berkshire population as a whole

- analysis of the number of admissions staying one night or zero nights only – could some sort of assessment centre save a number of inappropriate admissions (see Figure 7.3)?

- expenditure adjusted for age-weighted population, by practice

- emergency admissions year to date for two consecutive years (see Figure 7.4).

There is a wealth of information to be derived from the data sets provided to the project, in conjunction with data available within practice systems and other sources. Further work planned includes comparisons between the preparatory year and the live year in various areas to establish or confirm the changes that the project has brought about, and focusing in on particular disease areas such as asthma to determine whether some practices have lower referral rates and to promote discussion within the project on possible causes of differences, such as higher investment in asthma nurses in some practices than others.

Information about services currently being purchased for the practices within fundholding and non-fundholding can be analysed alongside data for the rest of the health authority population to determine differences in referral and treatment rates. Discussion of these differences with providers and the health authority can lead to planned changes in contracted levels and the introduction of quality clauses in contracts to reflect a planned change in clinical behaviour.

Looking to the future

GP-led purchasing at sub-health authority level, whether through total purchasing schemes or other types of locality based projects, needs good quality information to support decision making and to focus the minds of GPs to initiate changes in primary, community and secondary care. A comprehensive knowledge of what is happening now is needed prior to changes being initiated, and there is little point in attempting to engage a

Table 7.2: Top 20 diagnoses for non-elective episodes: April–September 1995

Practice 1		BIPP as a whole	
ICD 10	Diagnosis description	ICD 10	Diagnosis description
O021	Missed abortion	R104	Other and unspecified abdominal pain
I200	Unstable angina	J459	Asthma, unspecified
I48	Respiratory disorders in diseases classified elsewhere	I200	Unstable angina
I64	Dentofacial anomalies (including malocclusion)	O021	Missed abortion
I211	Acute transmural myocardial infarction of inferior wall	K529	Non-infective gastroenteritis and colitis, unspecified
I802	Phlebitis/thrombophlebitis, other deep vessels low extremities	Z488	Other specified surgical follow-up care
J90	Psoriasis	I64	Dentofacial anomalies (including malocclusion)
R073	Other chest pain	S7200	Fracture of neck of femur
R104	Other and unspecified abdominal pain	I209	Angina pectoris, unspecified
R55	Foreign body in respiratory tract	I48	Respiratory disorders in diseases classified elsewhere
S7200	Fracture of neck of femur	P071	Other low birthweight
I209	Angina pectoris, unspecified	I500	Congestive heart failure
O034	Spontaneous abortion, incomplete, without complications	R073	Other chest pain
R074	Chest pain, unspecified	S099	Unspecified injury of head
C509	Breast, unspecified	I802	Phlebitis/thrombophlebitis, other deep vessels lower extremities
I501	Left ventricular failure	R074	Chest pain, unspecified
J180	Bronchopneumonia, unspecified	I219	Acute myocardial infarction, unspecified
J449	Chronic obstructive pulmonary disease, unspecified	J181	Lobar pneumonia, unspecified
K529	Non-infective gastroenteritis and colitis, unspecified	N390	Urinary tract infection, site not specified
K566	Other and unspecified intestinal obstruction	I501	Left ventricular failure

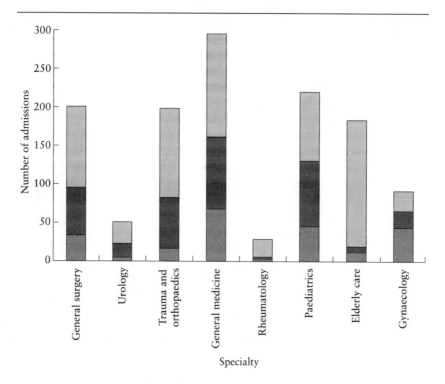

Figure 7.3: BIPP emergency admissions to Royal Berkshire and Battle Hospitals NHS Trust, April–August 1995, by length of stay group (major specialties only). Length of stay: (▢) = > 1 day; (■) = 1 day; (▤) = 0 days. Data from RBBH inpatient MDS.

practice in discussions about high referral rates if the GPs can immediately point to inaccuracies in the data. Good quality information, however, is not cheap, and this section seeks to show how costs might be reduced in the future without a reduction in data quality.

Most fundholding GPs have confidence in and ownership of the data held in fundholding systems, because these have been validated by practice staff against clinical information such as discharge letters.

However, data validation and manual entry into the fundholding systems is an extremely time-consuming and therefore expensive task. Even so, the fundholding systems are not well suited to providing information to inform GP decision making, because they are essentially accounting systems and do not hold the complete MDS.

For fundholding practices, management costs average about £50 000, and of this a substantial proportion would be devoted to data validation

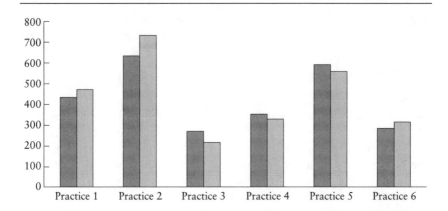

Figure 7.4: Royal Berkshire and Battle Hospitals NHS Trust emergency admissions, April–November 1995/6 (▢), compared with the same period in 1994/5 (■).

and data entry. Data entry and validation effort for the non-fundholding activity for the same practice would cost almost as much again. For all practices to have access to valid data about their utilization of health care services, the cost would amount to several millions of pounds in Berkshire alone. Given finite funding for the NHS, there is a dilemma here: validation of data by practice staff is required if data are to be believed by GPs, but the cost of this is excessive and must ultimately remove money from patient care.

The answer must surely be that the manual validation and data entry processes will increasingly need to be automated. The NHSE's IM&T strategy contains some initiatives that will significantly reduce manual effort needed to validate data. These initiatives include the following.

- *The NHS Administrative Register (NHSAR)* – This is a database containing patient demographic details derived from the FHSA Patient Register. Berkshire is a pilot site for the NHSAR, and the main acute provider in Reading is due to have access to the system. When it is fully linked with the Trust's own patient system, it should eliminate problems of the 'not our patient' variety.

- *Electronic data interchange* – The use of electronic discharge notification to practices will facilitate automated checking of data sets against discharge letters within the practice. This is currently one of the most labour intensive tasks in fundholding administration. Electronic input of patient data and invoices into fundholding systems is also being piloted at sites around the country.

Will health authorities still need to hold contract data sets for all of their population if contracts are managed at a locality or total purchasing level, given the duplication of data that arises? Without such health authority-wide databases, needs assessment and comparisons across larger populations will not be possible, and such systems could be used by total fundholding or locality projects as their principal means of contract monitoring and management, providing data were validated by practices. Ownership of the data by the GPs is paramount. Consideration is also needed of how the wealth of morbidity data available in practice systems can be made available for comparative needs assessment and planning of services.

In conclusion initiatives are being introduced that will eliminate many of the inefficiencies that currently beset fundholding administration. The challenge will be to integrate health authority and practice systems in a way that will preserve confidentiality, eliminate data duplication and fully support primary care-led purchasing. Health authorities and total purchasing projects will then have the tools and data needed for planning where to invest scarce health care resources to create the greatest health gain in the population.

8

Total purchasing – the acute Trust
Alan Hudson and
Alastair Mitchell-Baker

In an area where standard fundholding had been well taken up by a large number of local GPs, the extension of the scheme to cover total purchasing was the next logical step. The existing scheme allowed participating GPs to ignore the financial effects of emergency episodes and of referring patients to hospitals outside the district for more expensive care, which could be provided as effectively locally, where this fell outside fundholding. It was envisaged that total purchasing would encourage greater responsibility by the GPs for all their purchasing decisions, at the same time offering them more freedom in the treatment of their patients.

Strategic considerations for an acute Trust

The Royal Berkshire and Battle Hospitals NHS Trust was in the unusual position of having a veto on the development of total purchasing locally as the BIPP project was one of the first four pilots to be announced and the GPs agreed that they only wished to proceed if their major acute and community Trusts supported the idea in principle. Other Trusts will not have this luxury but will need to consider how much effort to put into supporting total purchasing. Our reasons for favouring the development of total purchasing were:

- recognition that, over time, GPs were going to be more involved in all purchasing decisions
- the need to work with the shift of work and resources to primary care rather than against it
- a relatively secure competitive position as potential competitors were at least 30 miles away and therefore we were able to size (up or down) according to real need in dialogue with GPs

- positive experience of standard fundholding in encouraging dialogue between GPs and consultants

- a move towards locality purchasing with an exception that BIPP GPs, although not a true locality, would behave as a locality purchasing group

- a need to tackle the problem of rising numbers of emergencies with GPs.

Our strategic decision has been reinforced by subsequent policy movements towards a primary care-led NHS and Berkshire Health Authority's decision to move to locality purchasing. For a Trust in a more competitive position, the need to work closely with a total purchasing pilot would be even clearer. The total purchasing pilot forms about 10% of the acute Trust's income, and we have a second smaller one going live in 1996/7.

Catalyst for change

The main motivation behind the involvement of all parties in total purchasing was the opportunity to improve upon the existing methods of purchasing and hence improve patient care. GP fundholders had made significant impact in elective surgery, outpatients and the direct access areas, and it was hoped that this largely beneficial influence could be extended across the whole hospital. Within the Trust it is important that all employees are working to a similar agenda, and the extension of the scheme provides an opportunity for the influence of GPs to extend into areas of care previously not covered by fundholding, for example maternity services and oncology.

One of the main driving forces of standard fundholding was the fact that for a GP, individual patients were important, whereas within a hospital waiting list the patient numbers were so large that the personal touch was sometimes omitted. Therefore in the same way that the existing fundholding scheme highlighted the individual patients of each practice within elective surgery, total purchasing would do the same for emergency admissions. As a result of this, the scheme could be used as a catalyst for initiating new methods of treatment and changing existing referral protocols.

Information

Total purchasing, as its name implies, covers all aspects of patient care. This extends the scheme to cover all areas of the hospital and as a consequence entails significantly greater quantities of data to be collected, from a wide range of new areas. In many cases the existing DHA contracts had not been sufficiently detailed to require this level of data collection. This required new disciplines for some departments unused to this level of detail, while they still provided their existing quality of clinical care. In many cases the new areas had been covered by a single block element of the local purchasing DHAs, but total purchasers would want more detailed cost and volume contracts, which they themselves would be monitoring in their practices, and could help us validate our data collection.

Data extension

The main areas that will require immediate additional resources will be the information and data collection areas, but they may also include additional administrative support for clinical staff in patient areas. Siting data collection systems in clinical areas should ensure that data collection is as accurate as possible and completed immediately following completion of the patient episode.

There will be many new areas of information required, including those that at present are not geared up to collect the quality and quantity of data involved, for example family planning clinics and A&E departments. This poses a training requirement so that the staff appreciate the importance of accurate data collection and understand that the Trust's income, the future success and ultimately their jobs depend on it. Many of the departments concerned – maternity, A&E, day care centres, family planning, etc. – have been protected from change in the first five years of the internal market by block contracts. However the GPs, with the departments concerned, can now look at ways in which significant changes in service provision can be achieved; for example the maternity department has recently given GPs and midwives direct access to induction for postmaturity, removing the need for an unnecessary outpatient appointment, and our A&E department has developed a clinical information system with excellent clinical letters to GPs, which were previously forgotten about, creating additional work for GPs and A&E officers as GPs tried to find out what treatment their patients had received in A&E. A side-effect of the high-quality letters is proper data collection. The practices have realized for the first time how much unnecessary work is being performed in the A&E department, and some of the total purchasing practices are developing alternative ways of dealing with this inappropriate A&E usage in primary care.

Data validation

Large quantities of data bring their own problems, not least that of validation: for example was the correct information recorded in the first place? This highlights an area that is in need of further development within contracting, that of clinical audit. This continues to be undertaken in many areas as a stand-alone task, divorced from all other contracting procedures. Checking data entry, and thus validating all casemix information, is a vital area as the contracting complexity increases. This then leads to various other questions of re-referral rates, outcome measures, etc. These need to play a part in longer-term strategic planning, and their current lack of use is causing a major problem to provider units that have to keep trying to achieve annual short-term priorities.

Data quantity and capture

The additional quantities of data will highlight a number of areas, one in particular being that data should be collected electronically, as close to the patient as is possible, and preferably while the patient is actually present. The modern desktop PC now has the capability to process the vast quantities of patient data. These data should then be available centrally to any other systems that may have a need to access them. Central validations can then be employed that are based upon not only common sense but also clinical logic, for example should this *man* be having an antenatal cytology test? Ideally over time we should move to linking acute Trust, community Trust, DHA and GP information systems, and as a byproduct of our total purchasing project we are working on such computer linking. This then is the 'vision of seamless health care' so often advocated by the NHS Information Management Group. Total purchasing can act as a catalyst for such change owing to its need for high-quality data interchange. Major benefits in terms of reduced transaction costs should accrue from the removal of duplication of data collection and validation by both the Trust and the GP practice, which happens at present. Accurate data collection by the Trust alone will be vital to achieve this.

GP/hospital liaison

One of the most important aspects of the total purchasing scheme for the newly involved areas of the Trust is to get the department concerned working with the GPs, to remove the 'fear factor', so that the true patient benefits can be realized. All change involves opportunities and threats, and a key task is to help departments to maximize the opportunities of total purchasing. There is no benefit in a total purchasing pilot making a short-term gain, at the expense of a whole hospital department, that is ultimately required to provide an ongoing service to the fundholder's patients. For example while in the short term it might be advantageous for a standard fundholder to take all his orthopaedics to the private sector, it might potentially damage his trauma service outside fundholding. The key in this situation is to work together responsibly, to achieve clearly identified changes that are in the interests of all patients. This has the effect of balancing increased risk with increased trust between GPs and hospital consultants and managers.

Many staff will have their working practices altered by the introduction of total purchasing. These personnel include contract monitoring staff and information department staff, as well as those staff who actually deal with the patients in a revised way. Total purchasing can have significant implications on the methods of referral, treatment and discharge of all patients, especially those requiring low-dependency care, some of whose care may be transferred into the community.

Developments such as hospital-at-home may well be developed by a Trust and a group of total purchasers as pilot schemes, which can ultimately, following a period of evaluation, be extended to all local GP practices.

The relationship between GPs and hospital consultants is very important, and this is where major changes in patient treatment methodology can be agreed and implemented. This involves both parties having a clear understanding of the patient benefits available and the implications of the changes on each other, and a strong desire to make the changes happen.

Risk assessment and change management

Even if the provider unit is supportive of the changes that are proposed by the GPs, there remains an element of risk. Some services, for example some maternity services as a result of the Changing Childbirth initiative, are moving to a community setting rather than being delivered in the district general hospital, as has happened historically. For this to take place there must be a period of adjustment for both the hospital and the community services, which may be resource intensive, especially during the pilot phase. In some cases the costs of community care may actually be higher than the costs of hospital care, but the outcomes, re-referral rates and quality of care for the patient may be much better. There may be a need for 'pump-priming' monies to be made available so that the hospital services can continue to operate for the rest of the population and so results of the pilot schemes can be evaluated before the situation is adopted on a wider basis.

As an example the Royal Berkshire Trust has recently developed a Changing Childbirth project with one of its total purchasing practices in which three midwives are attached to the practice, providing a 24-hour community midwifery service, accompanying patients to the labour ward and supervising their intrapartum care. In theory this releases core labour ward staff, but as the pilot only involves 120 deliveries *per annum* out of 5000 a year in the unit, the labour ward has to retain its full complement of staff. The project costs are therefore additional to the normal costs of running a maternity service. If the project were extended to other practices, core labour staff costs could be reduced as community costs increased.

Commissioning decision making

Front-line contracting and negotiating staff must have the right qualities, skills, knowledge and decision making capabilities so that they gain the confidence of GPs and practice managers. The development of clinical directorates has been crucial in allowing this to happen. Compared with health authorities, fundholders have been able to make faster decisions and stand by them. It is important that the problem of delays in decision making by health authorities are avoided as fundholding expands to approach the same scale as health authorities; many of the pilot schemes involve consortia of several practices and may have populations almost the size of small health authorities.

Effecting change

There are a number of major areas in which the GPs feel that they can significantly change the current working practices of their local district general hospital. These include:

- reduced numbers of emergency admissions – use of community support and hospital-at-home

- reduced length of stay – especially by improving discharge procedures

- removal of the simpler parts of the casemix – hospital becomes more a centre of specialization and excellence.

These will have significant effects on both the running of the hospital and the overall casemix, the latter becoming more complex. Average costs per episode may therefore increase as a result of the greater dependency of the patients requiring specialist care. In the long term, if the contraction of secondary care continues there will be significant changes within the district general hospitals as patients become more dependent on specialist care. It is obviously very important that a Trust works closely with all commissioners, especially GPs, who will have a strong interest in ensuring that the process does not go too far, leaving them without acute beds for admissions. Total purchasing offers a convenient and useful forum for this interface, and our experience has taught us that fundholders' concerns frequently mirror those of other GPs.

Contracting structure

In the early days of fundholding major problems were encountered by Trusts as they had to develop two incompatible pricing systems.

1 *Fundholding prices* – Within a specialty certain surgical procedures were priced individually. Realistic pricing was essential to prevent 'cherry-picking'. Fundholders would take procedures set at too high a price off to a new, possibly private, provider.

2 *DHA prices* – Each specialty had an average specialty price based upon assumed casemix. These prices completely ignore any effects of change in-year due to:

  - changes in clinical practice, for example shorter hospital stay
  - efforts by GPs to get patients out more quickly
  - changes in casemix – more or fewer complicated patients than expected.

Total purchasing made the scenario even more complex as the average specialty costs of total purchasing procedures outside standard fund-holding were different from the average specialty costs of procedures to the health authority. This potentially meant that a Trust needed three different pricing structures:

1 fundholding banded prices

2 health authority average specialty costs

3 total fundholding average specialty costs (excluding their separately set fundholding prices).

In order to reduce the complexity of pricing we decided to charge the authority fundholding prices for their non-fundholders, and average specialty costs excluding fundholding procedures for their non-fundholders and fundholders not involved in total purchasing. As the use of HRGs develops we expect to move to HRGs for fundholding and health authority prices.

Total purchasers were unwilling to accept average specialty costs for emergencies, as they expected to be pro-active in changing the delivery of patient care and wanted to see the benefits of reduced lengths of stay reflected in reduced prices and transfer of the resources saved to community services. Superficially it might appear that an acute Trust was damaging itself by agreeing to the abandonment of average specialty cost, but in practice there would have been huge risks to the Trust in retaining it as the GPs would have been tempted to 'cherry-pick' emergency admissions, dealing with the lower-dependency emergencies outside the acute Trust, leaving the acute Trust with a more complex casemix with an unrealistic (too low) average cost.

In any case NHS Trusts are obliged to move towards using HRGs as a contracting currency. Those involved with a total purchasing pilot may well want to move more quickly towards HRG pricing than is proposed by the national timescale.

We are also looking at the development of differential pricing for maternity by grading all our total purchasing pilot maternity patients into various degrees of complexity in different aspects of their maternity care (Figure 8.1).

Initially at least the health authority has kept its existing pricing structure, which means that as with standard fundholding and commissioning we have to maintain two different pricing structures, but over time the health authority is moving towards locality purchasing and will then presumably wish to move to the more sensitive pricing that we develop with our total purchasers.

Drawing up a balance sheet of the impact of total purchasing on the acute Trust

As we draw to the end of the first year of total purchasing, we can clarify the costs and benefits of total purchasing for an acute Trust.

HOSPITAL NUMBER			
WOMAN'S SURNAME		PATIENT LABEL	
GP & PRACTICE			
DATE DELIVERED		DATE DISCHARGED TO HEALTH VISITOR	
BOOKING CONSULTANT	☐ C		
MIDWIFE	☐ MW		
ANTENATAL OUTPATIENT	☐ ZERO	zero	referrals
REFERRAL	☐ LOW	1	referrals
	☐ MEDIUM	2	referrals
	☐ HIGH	>2	referrals
ANTENATAL ADMISSION	☐ ZERO	zero	days
	☐ LOW	1–3	days
	☐ MEDIUM	4–7	days
	☐ HIGH	>7	days
ANTENATAL COMMUNITY	☐ ZERO	Most of care out of the area	
CARE	☐ NORMAL	Normal number of visits	
		Normal care	
	☐ HIGH	Extra visits	
		Prevention of hospital admission	
		BP checks	
INTRA-PARTUM CARE	☐ ZERO	Delivered out of the area	
	☐ NORMAL	Normal delivery	
		Induction – arm	
	☐ MEDIUM	Forceps/ventouse	
		PPH	
		Induction – prostaglandins	
		Breech	
		Home delivery	
		Pool birth	
	☐ HIGH	LSCS	
POSTNATAL HOSPITAL	☐ ZERO	Did not deliver in the hospital	
CARE	☐ NORMAL	Normal baby	
		Less than 48 hour stay	
	☐ HIGH	48 hour + stay	
		Baby on Rushey (neonatal ward)	
POSTNATAL COMMUNITY	☐ ZERO	Most of care out of the area	
CARE	☐ NORMAL	Care 10 days or less	
		Normal care	
		Normal number of visits	
	☐ HIGH	Care more than 10 days	
		Feeding counselling	
		Wound infection	
		Broken down perineum	
		Extra visits	

Figure 8.1: Obstetrics costing information.

Positive impact of total purchasing

- Helped the Trust to develop information systems in areas such as maternity and A&E.

- Helped the Trust to develop more refined prices, for which sophisticated information is the key.

- Has begun to effect change in areas other than elective surgery and outpatients.

- Helped to explore the rise in the number of emergencies and how we can work together to tackle it.

- Opportunity to develop GP/consultant dialogue in new areas.

- Tough but fair contracting with rapid decision making about correction of an over-performing contract (arising because BIPP GPs were over-optimistic about their impact on emergency care).

Negative impact of total purchasing

- Costly in terms of better information, management time and effort, although this should reduce over time as proper systems feed through.

- Short timescale of project led to pressure to demonstrate change in unrealistic time limits.

- Pressure for rapid change, sometimes leading to an unhelpful confrontational stance, for example on economic pricing.

- Divergence from the health authority stance on some issues, for example family planning, which BIPP GPs wished to see moved into their practices, while the health authority wished to preserve the choice between our clinics and general practice. This should lessen as the health authority moves to primary care-led localities.

- Not always enough dialogue between GPs and consultants.

- Frustration that the artificial divide between total purchasing and GMS prevents the solution to clearly identified problems, for example the reluctance of practices to deal with huge inappropriate A&E usage identified by better information systems, as a resource shift into practices was not possible.

Conclusion

In conclusion the total purchasing scheme is acting as a catalyst in the development of the new primary care-led NHS. It is creating risks for the large provider unit but is also a positive way forward for the future. A number of alternative scenarios have been put forward for the district general hospital of the twenty-first century, which concur that the hospital will be smaller and more specialist, and involve a greater use of technology. Total purchasing is at the forefront of patient care from secondary to primary care, and is developing better community services based around the GP practice. This can be destabilizing for the hospital, and the role and responsibility of the GP fundholders and their willingness to compromise on the pace of change will determine the success of total purchasing in the development of the NHS. In essence total purchasing is the beginning of the future, and any acute hospital that wants to be involved in creating the future must be involved with total purchasers.

9

A priority care Trust perspective
Sharon-Esther Sloan

West Berkshire Priority Care Service NHS Trust is a large organization that provides a wide range of diverse services, including community hospitals, general community services, mental health services, hospital and community, and community based services for people with learning difficulties.

The Trust has good relationships with colleagues from the Royal Berkshire and Battle Hospitals Trust and with GPs, both fundholding and non-fundholding. This Trust is committed to the development of mental health and community services and sees the shift of resources from secondary to primary care as one of the ways forward. If the shift in resources is achieved in a planned and constructive way, the long-term viability of local services will be stronger. This is a view shared with our colleagues in the acute Trust.

As the drive for a primary care-led NHS moves forward, it is essential fully to involve GPs in the planning and use of resources. Many GP fundholders are frustrated by being accused of 'playing the system' and pushing more patients through as emergency rather than elective admissions, thus putting financial pressure onto the purchasing commission. This had led to some GP fundholders opting for the choice of total purchasing, which gives them total responsibility for purchasing care and also carries the financial risk. In Berkshire there has been demonstrable benefit from working relationships with GP fundholders. This has resulted in investment in community services, particularly in community nursing, and the step from traditional fundholding to total purchasing seemed a natural choice for some practices and was supported by the Trust.

Developing good working relationships

It is important to emphasize the good working relationships, as much of the preparatory year for the total purchasing pilot was about sharing knowledge between Trusts and GPs. Both Trusts are committed to reducing the length of stay for hospital patients and finding alternatives in the community to medical admissions. The development of local community hospital services is also an important area for GPs and the Trusts. If these aims are to be achieved, the changes must be properly planned; this is a concept shared by both the Trusts and the GPs. For total purchasing to succeed, evidence of good working relationships between Trusts and GPs is a necessary ingredient. No-one benefits from unplanned short-term change, and no Trust will enter willingly into a relationship that appears to threaten their services unless there is an acknowledgement of the necessity of managing change, whether this is potential downscaling or planning of developments.

Viewing total purchasing positively

From a priority care Trust's point of view, there are several areas that make total purchasing by GPs an attractive option. West Berkshire Priority Care Trust is committed to working with GPs and is keen to see primary care services enhanced and developed. The pressures regarding early hospital discharges and the ever-increasing demand for more care in a community setting under which GPs find themselves are very similar to those which community services like district nursing and physiotherapy are facing. Mental health services remain in the shadow of acute medical and surgical services as the drive continues to push down waiting times for operations such as hip replacement. The incentive here is that GPs become more aware of how many or how few resources are spent on mental health services, and a greater understanding of acute mental health services enables them to make sound local decisions.

The risk of total purchasing

The flip side of the argument for going forward with total purchasing from the Trust's view is the potential risk to clinical stability and the financial risk. It took some GP fundholders several years to understand how some services operated, what the impact of not having them would be or how they could best be developed for the future. There is always the possibility that GPs have unrealistic expectations of how quickly services can change. The time needed to understand services, such as long-stay inpatient care, in which they may have had little recent involvement must not be underestimated. Most GP fundholders did not make rapid change in their first year of fundholding, and one danger of total purchasing could be the pressure to deliver change quickly in a short timespan of a project. This is particularly concerning if the Trust is trying to move forward major strategic plans that have been on the table for some time with the host health authority.

Pressure for sensitive pricing by total purchasers

In order to release cash from secondary care, the GPs were very forceful in demanding changes in pricing structures from FCEs to bed days or a weighted alternative. Fortunately our Trust had already moved to pricing in bed days in most of our hospitals, and we only had to make this adjustment to one community hospital where the GPs wanted us to set up new GP medical beds. The GP medical beds were established with collaborative meetings to agree admitting protocols and clear statements that we were not in the 'business' of admitting acute medical patients who required district general hospital care. As this was a new service and it was difficult to gauge demand, we agreed to cost the additional work at marginal cost, with an agreement that if the demand for the service did not materialize, only the marginal variable cost would be at risk. This was a clear area of shared risk in developing a new service that is to date going well and is in increasing demand.

Information

One area that proved labour intensive and is still time-consuming is that of information. The GPs wanted the same level of validation and detail of information for non-fundholding services as they were used to for fundholding ones. The problem here was the historical underfunding of information systems and people. The project had funding built into it for additional resources to monitor and service the contract, and this is a vital area that should not be looked upon lightly, especially in community services where there are a limited number of computerized systems available. If the historical data used to set the base are poor, there will be difficulties in comparing the capitation budget allocation, and this could result in not enough money being contracted back to the Trust and windfall savings for the purchasers. In future years, if the data collection improved, the windfall savings will disappear and there will be the potential for an overspend by the purchasers.

Information to service contracts should ideally be obtained as a by-product of useful clinical data. We are working with one of our total purchasing practices to develop an interface between practice and Trust data that will result in contractual data being produced as a byproduct of clinical data collected by health visitors and district nurses.

Initial contract

The cost and volume contract was initially set for a period of six months with a 2% trigger based on the bottom line finance figure; i.e. if the financial figure went above or below 2%, financial rewards or penalties would be applied. The Trust would have preferred a 12 month contract, but the GPs were not sure how robust the data used to set the contract were, even though a full eight months' data had been validated. In some areas, particularly in preventative services such as health promotion, it was difficult to disaggregate information. GPs have historically not been involved with health promotion departments, and they are questioning the benefits the service brings in the way it is delivered at the moment. This is an ongoing debate, and the Trust is looking at ways of meeting the GP purchasers' needs as well as the health authority's wider remit of purchasing health promotion for the local population.

At the end of the six months an additional six months' activity was contracted for. Some fundholders work almost entirely using cost per case contracts, which would prove difficult with total purchasing, where the financial risk would be large. The short timespan of the project probably contributed to the short-term contract but is not something that reduces the perceived financial risk for Trusts. As total purchasers move from shorter timescale horizons of fundholding to a longer-term strategic approach, we would like to see the development of longer three- to five-year rolling contracts to help planning.

Hospital-at-home

GPs, like community staff, are well aware of the increasing pressures on them from early hospital discharge and care in the community. There has been no growth in community nursing in our Trust over the last few years other than from fundholding practices. The Trust recognizes that there is an opportunity to work with GPs in total purchasing to develop hospital-at-home. The Trust has discussed this with the GPs, and a working group with a nominated GP and a representative from the health authority has been set up to take the project forward.

Involving staff in total purchasing

It is important that all staff are aware of and understand the implications of total purchasing. GPs' needs and wants may differ from those of the host purchaser, and this often requires innovation and flexibility in meeting their needs. Total funds usually involve large sums of income for Trusts, and staff need to understand the different pressures that total purchasing can bring to them with a whole new set of purchasers.

GP fundholding and total purchasing

It is not easy neatly to separate fundholding and total purchasing as some of the changes from fundholding can easily impact on services outside fundholding. This may be true in community nursing: many fundholders have invested additional money into nursing, and this may mean greater community support for their patients, which could be linked to reduced hospital admissions and give more flexibility in arranging hospital discharge for patients.

Conclusions

The main benefits of the project have been greater GP involvement in wider issues of purchasing, the encouragement of collaboration between secondary and primary care and raised awareness of services outside fundholding. The main concerns are about the possible short-term view and rush to achieve objectives, and the difficulty in achieving joint purchasing decisions between GPs and the host purchaser to ensure a consistent approach to service development.

Key points to note in total purchasing

- Collect as much relevant information as is possible.
- Get staff on board and keep them informed.
- Build on good relationships with purchasers.
- Nominate a senior member of staff to service the contract.
- Allow time for GPs to get to know services with which they have not historically been involved.

10

Social services and total purchasing
Mike Powell

The relationship between doctors and social services assumes particular importance for the success of any total purchasing scheme. This has become of even greater significance with the government's promotion of community care. Most health authorities have formal arrangements with their local social services departments to clarify each body's responsibility for the provision of care; these agreements are often updated annually.

Organizational comparison

There are some important differences in the style of operation between social services and health authorities which are summarized in Table 10.1. It is important to understand the different structures as they have a profound influence on negotiations. For example a social services director may be quite happy to assume responsibility for providing a service but could find that this is blocked by the social services committee made up of elected councillors. Similarly transferring some services once provided by health authorities to social services may result in a previously free service being charged to the recipient.

Table 10.1: Differences in style of operation

Health authority	Social services
Quango – members tend to reflect the politics of the government	Answerable to locally elected councillors, who may not reflect government or may have no political majority
All services purchased free to patients	May charge for services and means test
Budget funded by central government	Budget partly central government grant, partly from rates. May be rate capped

Creating good relationships

Historically relationships between GPs and social services have not always been cordial. This has partly been caused by a lack of contact and partly by the very different training and *modus operandi* of the two professions. Social workers tend to work in teams and have less individual responsibility for their clients; doctors often feel that the social services response to sudden domestic crises, especially out of hours, is too slow to be of any practical use – for example in stepping in to look after a disabled person whose carer is unexpectedly hospitalized. Conversely social workers often feel that doctors are difficult to approach and are sometimes unhelpful in sharing information.

For total purchasing to be a success, these barriers must be broken down. This can be done at practice level by having practice attached social workers. The problem with this is that social services areas do not correspond to practice areas – our practice deals with five different social service offices in two counties. This will worsen with the establishment of unitary authorities; in Berkshire this will mean the replacement of one county-wide authority with six separate social service departments. At top level it is essential to have a senior social services officer involved as a member of the team running the scheme. As always understanding each other's problem makes for better co-operation. However, having the budget for community care divided artificially between 'social care' and 'health care' makes for difficulties in establishing the dream of a seamless service for patients and clients. Few people fit neatly into the 'social' or 'health' pigeon holes as most people have a mixture of social and health problems, and which one is predominant may vary on a daily or weekly basis.

This is at the root of many of the tensions between health authorities and social services and will naturally also concern total purchasing GPs.

Agreement between total purchasing group and social services headings

The areas to consider are:

1 define population covered by agreement

2 nursing homes for elderly

3 hospital nursing beds

4 day hospitals and day care

5 draft guidance on continuing care

6 elderly residential care

7 preserved rights

8 social services-purchased home care

9 community nursing/community intervention

10 care packaging

11 medical loans/occupational therapy equipment

12 learning disabilities

13 mental health

14 joint funding

15 palliative care

16 hospital discharge arrangements

17 assurance of no unilateral withdrawal of service

18 arbitration procedure.

This list may appear daunting, but it is important that everything is covered as agreeing policy at the outset is a lot easier than is subsequent argument.

The author does not propose to deal with all of these headings. Some, for example resettling long-stay psychiatric patients in the community, are difficult to influence as a total purchaser as they are part of a long-term strategy.

Nursing homes for the elderly (item 2)

Perhaps the more important area to influence is elderly care. The number of elderly people is growing rapidly; unfortunately severe disability is associated directly with increased age. Care in the community is a laudable concept but it is not cheap, and many people have to be cared for in nursing homes. The balance has to be struck between these two concepts of care.

Those people who are funded by social services may still have to have some care needs funded by the NHS. A list of these needs should be agreed with social services. Such a list may include:

• nasogastric/gastrostomy feeding

- mental health deterioration or behaviour problems

- specialist palliative care

- hemiplegic states and multiple sclerosis.

This list is just an example.

Likewise some specialist equipment may be the responsibility of the NHS, for example:

- specialist beds and mattresses

- oxygen equipment and nebulizers

- syringe drivers.

Discussion should also centre on the availability and standards of provision. A key to moving patients out of hospital is the ready supply of nursing home beds.

Hospital nursing beds (item 3)

The usage of beds in community hospitals should be examined. In some cases these beds may be inefficiently utilized. There is great potential for these beds to be used for patients who have only nursing needs, who all too often currently end up in a high-tech bed on a medical ward. The use of local beds is also popular with patients and relatives. In addition they can be cost effective as long as the pricing structure has been properly agreed.

Draft guidance on continuing care (item 5)

The financing of nursing home care is a minefield. A recent document from the Department of Health on NHS responsibilities for meeting continuous care needs states that 'the NHS has a clear responsibility to arrange and fund services to meet the needs of people who require continuing health care'. Criteria should be developed locally to define those people who should receive free NHS care.

It is very difficult to draw up unambiguous criteria, and the system does not really cater for patients whose status changes. Patients may enter a nursing home under the auspices of social services with mainly nursing needs and then become profoundly ill and in need of medical attention. This change in status will not be reflected by a change in the funding source.

That fact that social services funding is means tested can be very unfair to the spouse of a patient as savings above £10 000 are expected to be used for care. The spouse of a patient who requires long-term care could see him or herself reduced to penury as £10 000 will not sustain them for long and many spouses may survive for 15–20 years. The system also discourages the elderly from having savings and is the main reason why so many relatives fight so hard to have their need classified as being 'health'.

It is hard not to conclude on looking around nursing homes that a substantial number of the inmates should in fact have their care provided by the NHS by virtue of their condition, as in reality these homes are merely the re-provision of geriatric wards in the community. As a total purchaser it is not of course in one's interest to adopt such sentiments. This conundrum bedevils the provision of seamless service.

Appeals mechanism

There must be a clearly defined appeals mechanism whereby clients and patients can appeal against the classification of their needs being social rather than medical. Ideally this should provide a rapid solution to any dispute. Any tardiness would further hamper an already cumbersome system.

Limitations of care packaging (item 10)

Most care managers should be authorized to be able to commit expenditure for care up to a certain value per week without having to seek higher authority. Locally this is at present set at £200. There should also be an agreement to limit the total cost of care for any one client. There is a point at which community care, however desirable, may become unaffordable for an individual; this limit should be defined in the agreement.

Medical loans/occupational therapy equipment (item 11)

This is a crucial area. Patients are often prevented from being discharged from hospital or being cared for at home by the lack of provision of an essential piece of equipment. This may be a stairlift, a hoist or a special bed. Failure to provide these items can be hugely expensive in terms of extra hospitalization. There should be an efficiently maintained jointly funded system for medical equipment.

Mental health (item 13)

A joint statement is needed outlining the actions to be taken by social services and the purchasers. This needs to take note of the relevant legislation:

- 1948 National Assistance Act
- 1983 Mental Health Act and Code of Practice
- 1984 Police and Criminal Evidence Act
- 1986 Disabled Persons Act
- 1990 NHS and Community Care Act.

One should also take into account various government documents:

- Health of the Nation Key Area Handbook
- Care Programme Approach
- Care of the Severely Mentally Ill
- Supervision Registers
- Inter Agency Working Guidance.

Purchasers should be involved in the planning of strategy with mental health care Trusts. GP purchasers are in a good position to advise as they have everyday first-hand experience of the problems.

A key issue is the ready availability of properly trained psychiatric social workers, especially out of hours. This also applies on the health side to the provision of properly trained doctors (approved section 12 doctors).

The placement of many long-term institutionalized patients in the community requires multiagency co-operation.

Hospital discharge arrangements (item 16)

This is another key area. Standards should be set for the timeliness of the assessment. All long-stay patients should be regularly monitored to ensure that discharge is not being delayed because of a lack of an essential piece of equipment or a service. Lack of nursing home places can also be a factor.

GPs should *always* be consulted about discharge arrangements, and this must be written into the agreement.

Innovation

Because total purchasing does not include the social services budget, innovation will only be achieved by negotiation. There is scope for achieving change, especially in areas in which service provision may be duplicated.

A novel scheme has been set up by Balmore Park Surgery in Caversham, Berkshire. The surgery has employed an occupational therapist, and the social services department has agreed to allow her to access its resources when needed. This is a win–win situation as social services gain by relieving pressure on their overstretched occupational therapists, and the patients gain by having speedier access to resources.

There might be scope for cutting down the numbers of different personnel visiting the same patient if more flexible working practices could be adopted.

Emergency social care teams might be able to obviate some acute admissions. However, the cost of the team would be borne by social services, while the benefits in terms of reduced expenditure would fall to the NHS purchaser. The solution might be to share those savings, but that is not straightforward as there are financial rules governing how health authorities may spend their money, and purchasing social care is *ultra vires*.

The saga of the ceiling tracks – a cautionary anecdote

Mr Biggs is a 68-year-old man with advanced multiple sclerosis. He is unable to weight-bear and was in a rehabilitation ward at the local acute Trust hospital. His wife would be able to manage him at home if she were able to move him from his bed to the toilet. A hoist system with rails suspended from the ceiling is available, but before this can be installed an occupational therapist from the social services department needs to assess him and his house. Occupational therapists are in short supply, and Mr Biggs' assessment was delayed. The provision of equipment and modification of the house is funded by a grant from the local district council; if they had run out of money, no grant would have been forthcoming until the next financial year, but money was fortunately available for Mr Biggs. However, the onus is on the family to employ a builder to do the modifications. A builder agreed to do the work on a set date, but when the time came he did not show up – he had gone out of business. Eventually the work was done and Mr Biggs was taken home.

However, this process took 9 months, and for 6 months of this time Mr Biggs was ready for discharge. The cost of his rehabilitation bed was £66 000 pounds; the cost of the work to be done was only £15 000. This bureaucratic delay left the health authority paying £42 000 unnecessarily. It would have been cheaper to have paid for the work to be done themselves, but this would have been a misapplication of funds.

The moral of this tale is that total purchasers must work with all other agencies to streamline bureaucratic procedures to ensure minimum delay. It is the total purchaser who will watch the 'taxi meter' clocking up the cost, and the patient and the nation who lose out.

Remember:

Streamlining bureaucracy costs little but yields much.

Summary

- Establish good relationships with the social services department.

- Develop an understanding of its political system and local problems.

- Try to get a senior officer involved with the total purchasing group.

- Draw up a joint plan with social services detailing your respective responsibilities.

- Jointly look at areas of duplication and waste.

- Set up an efficient medical equipment and loans system.

- Try and get staff on the ground to work together to maximize their potential.

- *Innovate* – but he prepared to drop innovations that do not work.

- Campaign politically for a more just system for long-term care.

11

Evaluation of total purchasing

Jonathan Shapiro and Nicola Walsh

In any sphere of life the evaluation of an experiment involves forming judgements about the appropriateness of an intervention and assessing whether the outcomes of the experiment are justified by the inputs. Evaluation is vitally important in providing solid evidence to inform future work, whether it be further research, practice or strategic policy. In the case of the BIPP, the specific purposes of the evaluation were to assess the costs and benefits attributable to the extension of GP fundholding to cover all areas of health care. The evaluation was also intended to inform any future approaches to commissioning, since BIPP, like the other three original pilot projects in Bromsgrove, Runcorn and Worth Valley, is determining its own 'rules of engagement' locally and without any central guidance.

Background

In the original General Practitioner Fundholding Scheme one of the key objectives was to give GPs more control of resources for their patients. It was intended that these could be used to develop services within their practices to the benefit of their patients or to contract for the provision of more consumer sensitive services from other health care sectors. Both these possibilities were felt to be pertinent to the central aim of improving 'the quality of services on offer to patients'.[1] The original scheme was restricted to practices with lists of greater than 11 000 patients; the secondary care services covered were confined to specified 'cold' surgical procedures, most (but not all) outpatient services and diagnostic services, and there was an expenditure ceiling of £5000 per patient above, after which practices were to approach their DHA for funding.

The reasons for these original restrictions probably related to concerns about:

• the financial risk of a small population based fund

- the equitable distribution of health care resources
- possible disruption to existing structures in a 'steady state' first year.

Some initial evaluations of GP fundholding, while perhaps encouraging of the overall experiment, suggested that little had changed in the patterns of referrals between primary and secondary care and only small changes had occurred in prescribing patterns.[2]

Anecdotal reports and reports of surveys of fundholders have suggested that a lot more change occurred than has yet been reported from detailed studies of the scheme.[3] Critics of the scheme suggested that this apparent lack of effect on patterns of care was evidence that the scheme made no difference. Others, however, argued that any effects on patterns of care could only be expected to emerge over a longer period of time.

The evidence from Glennerster's more recent work suggests that the anticipated changes to patterns of care are beginning to occur in the fundholders he has been studying.[4]

It may be that the goal of increased sensitivity of secondary care provision to patients' needs (as perceived by GPs) is being realized only slowly because of the initial restrictions placed on the fundholding scheme.

Studies of fundholding to date have failed to show its anticipated negative effects. Concerns about the emergence of a two-tier system continue to be expressed but evidence of this is, in the main, equivocal. Some commentators argue that even if it does occur it will only be a transitional effect.[5]

Evidence of damage to the doctor/patient relationship (from a conflict of interest between the two) as anticipated by Drummond has not generally been detected, although whether patient satisfaction is more generally waxing or waning is disputed.

Selection of patients in relation to the financial risk they pose to the fund has also been suggested, but evidence has not been formally reported.[6] Finally, the fear that GPs might not be able to cope with the managerial requirements of the scheme have proven unfounded, although the considerable ongoing financial and personal costs to the GPs involved in the scheme have become more apparent, and doubts are emerging about whether these can be sustained.

The extension of GP fundholding to cover the complete range of health care services and to give GPs more scope to mould services for their patients enabled us to assess some of the concerns expressed above. The purchasing of all hospital and community care services by groups of GPs is an important development in the NHS reforms. Its impact on the internal market, its acceptability to GPs and its effect on patient care all needed careful assessment.

The national evaluation programme

In March 1995 the Department of Health announced an independent national evaluation of all 53 total purchasing schemes in England and Scotland. The research is being carried out by a consortium of seven research institutes led by the King's Fund Institute. This evaluation is intended to focus on the implementation and impact of the total purchasing pilot schemes. Information will be collected on:

- the factors associated with successful set-up and operation of total purchasing
- the costs and effectiveness of total purchasing compared with health authority purchasing in the context of ordinary GP fundholding
- the benefits to patients of total purchasing compared with health authority purchasing in the context of ordinary GP fundholding.

This evaluation study will be based on a single set of criteria to ensure that the purchasing model is rigorously tested for its ability to provide:

- value for money
- health benefits
- improved patient satisfaction.

Although the four 'pioneer' total purchasing schemes are notionally included in the national evaluation study, each had already commissioned its own independent evaluation study before the national programme was devised. Consequently fieldwork and data in these four sites will be more detailed and intensive than will be possible in the other 49 sites participating in the national programme (the 'second wave' total purchasers).

It is worth adding at this point that, apart from the 53 projects cited above, many other local projects are being set up to look at all aspects of local commissioning. They range from other total purchasing experiments, through extended multifunds and locality commissioning projects, to 'locally sensitive purchasing' and locality planning projects. Some are led by GPs, others by health authorities and still more by partnerships of the two. Although some of them are being formally evaluated, there is a risk that many *ad hoc* schemes may be set up with little or no evidence of their effectiveness or otherwise.

The 'pioneer' evaluation studies

The four sites at Bromsgrove in Worcestershire, BIPP in Berkshire, Castle-fields in north Cheshire, and Worth Valley in North Yorkshire, all pion-eered the concept of total purchasing. The schemes evolved from local GPs taking forward the initiative in conjunction with civil servants at the NHS Executive. These were thus largely self-selected sites, and eligibility crite-ria were not applied.

Such criteria have, however, now been set for the second wave total purchasers, so the comparability of research findings between the first and second wave projects will need to be treated carefully. The evaluations of the four pioneer sites will be particularly valuable because of their extra detail, which will allow them to explore in more depth the complex inter-related issues involved in the commissioning and purchasing of health care services from a primary care base.

Before looking more closely at the evaluation of the BIPP, a brief out-lines of all the case studies is provided to illustrate the nature of the approaches being undertaken.

Bromsgrove

The small town of Bromsgrove forms an ideal locality in which to carry out a total purchasing experiment: there are four fundholding practices covering the whole of the town's population of about 40 000, a choice of both acute and community providers and health authorities (both FHSA and DHA, supported by the West Midlands RHA) that were prepared to invest human and financial resources in the project. The Bromsgrove experiment is being evaluated by a team from St Mary's Medical School in London.

Castlefields

Unlike the other three projects, the Runcorn project covers a single prac-tice with around 12 000 patients. The evaluation of the Castlefields pro-ject is being undertaken by Professor Margaret Pearson of the Health and Community Care Research Unit, Liverpool University.

Worth Valley

This project is made up of a consortium of eight practices covering a population of 66 000 people. The project aims to develop GP-led, locality based purchasing within the overall commissioning framework of Bradford Health Authority. The Consortium is being evaluated by Jenny Jefferson and Maxine Craven of the Nuffield Institute for Health in Leeds.

BIPP

The main purpose of the BIPP evaluation study is to assess whether the objectives set by the BIPP project board are being achieved. The evaluation is comparing purchasing and commissioning amongst the BIPP GPs and the activities undertaken at local health authority level.

The Health Services Management Centre (HSMC) at the University of Birmingham is already involved in the assessment of several locality purchasing projects around the country, which involve both fundholding and non-fundholding arrangements. It is anticipated that this other work will be used informally to inform comparisons of total purchasing against other commissioning models.

The BIPP study addresses issues of effectiveness, efficiency and acceptability in a way mirrored by the national evaluation programme.

- *Effectiveness* – Benefits to patients accruing from any changes that may occur in the delivery of community based and hospital care are being measured to assess the effectiveness of this model of purchasing.

- *Efficiency* – In determining efficiency the evaluation is looking at any benefits in relation to their costs. These include the direct financial costs of services delivered and the costs of managing those services, and the indirect costs to patients and their carers, GPs and their staff, and health service managers.

- *Acceptability* – To assess the acceptability of total purchasing, information from all the stakeholders is being collected at intervals to detect any changes in philosophy and delivery of the NHS as 'a universally available service, free at the point of use and providing services of the same high quality to all in order of priority of clinical need'. The stakeholders include patients, carers, GPs, other primary care workers in the NHS and other organizations such as social services, secondary care providers and management.

In principle effectiveness should be measured by assessing any improvement in population health that may be linked to the effects of total purchasing. However, there are three reasons why it will prove difficult to measure such improvements directly.

- The preservation of traditional funding mechanisms: Hospital and Community Health Service (HCHS) funds may not easily be invested in practice-provided services, and General Medical Services funds may not be used to fund non-GMS areas, so the potential for radical health promoting shifts in services may be hard to realize.

- Much of the care provided in the community sector is concerned with health maintenance or even with the minimization of health loss, as in people with long-term chronic illness; it is really more about *care* than about *cure*, so the traditional measures of cure may not be appropriate.

- The timescale of the formal project and its evaluation is too short to demonstrate any genuine changes in health status, particularly if we are hoping to show a causal link to the project. If the timescale were to be extended, it would become more feasible to show a change in health outcome.

In the interim much of the effectiveness of the project is being assessed by a review of processes, such as:

- referral and investigation patterns
- development and implementation of purchasing plans
- quality standards set in contracts
- prescribing patterns where appropriate
- balance between

    - BIPP priorities and health authority strategy
    - BIPP and national priorities

- the role of the health authority
- the role of the central BIPP office
- project implementation

    - budget setting
    - arrangements for contracting
    - resource inputs in

        (i)   the practices
        (ii) the central office
        (iii) the providers
        (iv) the health authority

- the management of risk by the practices and the providers
- the accountability arrangements

- impact on providers.

The evaluation study is also documenting the operating costs, the process of budget management (underspends and overspends), the management requirements and the use of savings.

In measuring any direct benefits of the project to patients in the present timescale, the evaluation is having to focus on process issues such as the impact of waiting times and access to primary and secondary care. The difficulty of measuring patient satisfaction is also not underestimated. Fitzpatrick[7] recommends devising measures specific to a purpose and concentrating only on the dimensions pertinent to that purpose. For this study we are concentrating on:

- patients' satisfaction with individual encounters with services in both primary and secondary care

- patients' perceptions of the acceptability and accessibility of the services on offer

- the apparent integration of the services.

The evaluation is also tracing emergency admissions rates, the use of accident and emergency services, relationships with social services, and patient transport services. In addition we will be tracking certain patient groups through their contacts with the health service, to determine a more global measure of the impact of the extension of standard fundholding.

The approach adopted in our study has been to start with some very broad qualitative questions; in the course of the fieldwork these questions have become more specific and focused and are being used to 'diagnose' the impact of the total purchasing scheme. In parallel to this qualitative approach, the activity data have been regularly collected and collated, so that quantitative information is available to consolidate and validate our findings (see below).

Data collection methods

Widening the scope of fundholding may be expected to generate changes in the structures, processes and possibly outcomes of health care in Berkshire. As changes will occur at many levels, so the relationships between them will need to be teased out. A simple framework of structure, process and outcome has been chosen as a tool to facilitate both the collection and collation of data and their interpretation.

A distinctive feature of case study research is the use of multiple methods and sources of evidence to establish validity. Case studies often use triangulation. In triangulation all data items are corroborated from at least one other source and normally by another method of data collection. Our study uses interviews and non-participant observation in combination with several different quantitative sources of data to establish an overall picture. The goal of qualitative research is to give emphasis to the meanings, experiences and views of all participants. It will contextualize the quantitative data that are collected.

Action research

In the hurly burly of rapid and continuous change in the NHS, it is essential that any research is both innovative and pragmatic so that managers and professionals are all fully engaged and accommodated in the process. As the 'rules of engagement' are being negotiated and agreed locally, it is also important to recognize the importance of the political and organizational context in which the schemes are located. An 'action research' approach, marrying the disinterested academic objectivity of an independent assessor with a careful input into the project management process, allows the project to be modified and developed as it runs and the impact of such modifications to be included in the final evaluation report.

Progress reports are provided to the BIPP project board at monthly intervals. The participants are thus kept informed about the progress of the evaluation study. Preliminary analyses are also shared at regular intervals with research participants, so the boundaries between researchers and researched become slightly blurred.

Such an approach is able to increase knowledge about total purchasing and to promote change in practice and delivery. It also enables closer relationships to be established between researchers and the project players so that the findings of the research are understood and incorporated locally and not just documented in a final report.

Conclusion

At the time of writing, BIPP and its evaluation have not been running long enough for any definitive and generalizable lessons to have emerged.

However, it is becoming clear that the methodology used in the evaluation, and particularly the combination of qualitative and quantitative methods, is very sensitive, signalling events and developments in a highly significant way and helping to shape the future of the project in a manner that does not threaten the objectivity of the assessment.

The evaluation of BIPP presents a rare opportunity for researchers to have an input at the 'coal face' of a project as well as at the policy level. Too often a 'top-down' model of the policy process is mirrored by a top-down model of the research process. This 'bottom-up' research process fits in well with the current trends towards a more devolved, locally sensitive health care system, which encourages more stakeholder involvement and has room for a variety of delivery models that will meet the distinct needs of different groups in a range of ways.

Promoting a dialogue between all the research units involved in the different evaluation studies of total purchasing will also be important if we are to maximize our understanding of this particular model of purchasing and fully inform future policies.

References

1 Department of Health (1990) *Practice budgets for general medical practitioners. Working paper 3*. HMSO, London.
2 Coulter A and Bradlow J (1993) Effects of NHS reforms on general practice referral patterns. *British Medical Journal*. **306**: 433–7.
3 Glennerster H, Matsaganis M and Owens P (1992) *A foothold for fundholding*. King's Fund Institute, London.
4 Glennerster H (1993) *Are GPs or districts better contractors?* King's Fund Institute, London.
5 Whitehead M (1993) Is it fair? Evaluating the equity implications of the NHS reforms. In: Robinson R, Le Grande J (eds) *Evaluating the NHS Reforms*. King's Fund Institute, London.
6 Crump B, Cubbon JE, Drummond MF *et al.* (1991) Fundholding in general practice and financial risk. *British Medical Journal*. **302**: 1582–4.
7 Fitzpatrick R (1992) Surveys of patient satisfaction: important general considerations. In: *Audit in action*. BMJ Publishing Group, London.

12

An alternative model – developing total purchasing in Wiltshire and Bath

Stephen Henry and Lesley Morris

Developing total purchasing in Wiltshire and Bath

In February 1994, as a result of attending a conference given by the four original total purchasing projects, we discovered that a neighbouring practice had already approached our commission (as it was then known) and opened negotiations. Combining forces we made a joint approach to the commission with a further two experienced fundholding practices from Bath and Frome. This provided a unique mix of four practices from three different FHSAs (Wiltshire, Avon and Somerset) with sufficient numbers (a combined list of 60 000) to join the second wave of pilots.

Our approach was that the four practices should remain independent with individual budgets but combine for risk and a joint agreement to adhere to the commission's ongoing strategy and funding mechanisms. One of the key strengths was the availability and accuracy of information about individual patients as opposed to population based public health data, which would give the commission a lever for change previously unavailable to them and a tool with which to persuade the providers to streamline and re-engineer their services. All were interested and co-operative, particularly a community Trust who realized the potential to enhance the role of several community hospitals previously under threat of closure.

Our own practice partnership had mixed views, several being justifiably wary of additional work-load pressures but appreciative of the opportunity for self-determination, to shift real resources from secondary to primary care and, unlike fundholding, be rewarded for their efforts.

Project framework

The steering group of authority executive directors, project co-ordinator and practice representatives:

- meets three-monthly
- oversees the project's development and management
- resolves policy issues.

The joint working group comprises a project co-ordinator (Chair), a manager and doctor from each practice, directorate members from the authority, i.e. finance, information, public health, etc. as appropriate to the agenda. The group:

- meets monthly
- processes operational management – the project plan
- develops a work programme to a realistic timetable
- integrates the programme into the business processes of the authority
- provides a regular forum for discussion, innovation and resolution of issues
- reports to the steering group
- assures that communication to all parties is maintained
- makes things happen.

The project co-ordinator is a member of the authority staff, jointly appointed by the practices and the authority to co-ordinate rather than manage the project. Each practice manages its own affairs.

Provider meetings

Regular meetings are held with the main Trusts shared by all four practices – acute (Royal United Hospital, Bath) and community (Wiltshire Health Care and Bath and West Community) and Bath Mental Health.

Topic meetings

Specific topics are covered in greater detail, for example:

- information

- contracting

- budget setting.

All key personnel from the authority, Trusts and practices are invited to these.

Management allowance

Each practice had an initial management allowance of £35 000 to support the pilot. This was to cover:

- enhanced computer software

- additional staff – management, administrative and clerical

- additional doctor time

- training

- support services – postage, telephone, fax, stationery, etc.

The rules for using the allowance were to be the same as those for fundholding. We have agreed that from the year 1996/7, the management overheads will be contained within the budget or, as the authority suggests, 'be covered by improved efficiency in contracting or a first charge against savings arising'!

Strategic framework

Unlike fundholding with a devolved budget for which the practices are separately accountable, total purchasing means that the practices are acting as agents of the health authority and so within the authority's ongoing agreed strategic framework. This provides a bonus, for the practices have now to be involved in the formative stage of the development of the authority's strategy. We are required to approve the business plans submitted by local Trusts and to join in the quarterly reviews of provider performance as serious players. Thus we have a major influence as a minority shareholder in the development of local health services. The authority says that it wishes to learn from our experience and incorporate these lessons in its own purchasing plans.

Fund allocation

We would have preferred to start with a weighted capitation formula, but acknowledge as experienced fundholders that we are now all below-average spenders. Second, we had agreed to share only our percentage of the purchasing element of the commission's funds and waive our interest in their overheads (management costs, reserves, etc.). This means that our budget income derives solely from existing contracts that have to be dis-aggregated from our individual practice percentage. This can only be done by calculating:

• historical information – (activity × average specialty cost) – where available, and for a complete year, or

• apportionment on an appropriate population share where activity information is unavailable or unreliable, or less than 1 episode per 1000 population. For example the family planning budget is apportioned across the registered 15–45-year-old female population rather than the total population.

A major concession is that the data can be practice/provider agreed rather than those from the authority. Currencies must remain consistent for calculation purposes, even if changed for contracting reasons.

There is to be a move to equity over four years on a 'fair shares for all practices' basis, i.e. from resource allocation methodology to weighted capitation as the national formula to effect this becomes more robust at practice level. 1995/6 budgets vary and lie between 10 and 23% lower than the weighted capitation calculations. Subsequent years will be based on GP fundholder cash rollover principles, uplifted for inflation, growth (+/–), changes in list size and progress to capitation, so it is imperative that the original fund base is as accurate as possible. The pilot is expected to provide the same level of efficiency savings as does the authority.

The major drawback of this allocation method is that the practices, unlike the commission, have no spare funds – every penny is 'expected' back by providers in return for continuation of activity levels. Funding for cash releasing savings (CRS), risk premium and proper support for primary care's extra work-load (nurse and doctor time), or further development, is estimated at around 5%. This can only be found by serious disinvestment in secondary services or an even bigger shift to primary care, exacerbating the problem.

Contracting

Having produced a list of what we knew we would be purchasing under total purchasing, we chose the areas where we would be:

- contracting 'live' for services – the majority of services provided at the local acute and community Trusts

- 'piggy backing' the authority's contract for services such as school medicals, transport, and drug and alcohol services – our identified percentage of each of these services remains part of the authority's current contract until we have unpicked and understood the activity

- 'blocking back' or remaining an integral part of the commission's contract, for example neonatal, special care and other very low-volume, high-cost services

- fixed price, non-attributable contracts to be used for highly confidential services, for example genitourinary medicine and family planning.

A condition of our becoming a pilot was to investigate the causes for the rise in emergency admissions in detail at practice level. We also agreed to look at community care locally to encompass the social service/community care interface. This would be helpful to the authority.

The authority's purchasers were concerned about the Trust's ability to produce the required information and costs. Extracting the practice's percentage from existing contracts would weaken the risk pool. We assured them that in year one, 1995/6, we would support existing contracts with our share, where appropriate, and follow the national guidelines on contracting.

Accountability

The accountability and monitoring processes follow the accepted fund-holding framework, incorporated with the authority's business planning cycle. The critical time points are:

- early summer – jointly to develop (together with other fundholders and GPs) the commission's strategic direction and purchasing plans

- end of November – submission of draft health plans and purchasing strategy

- January – evaluation and feedback to individual fundholders
- February – submission of final health plans
- monthly activity and financial reports
- quarterly contract performance reviews
- end of year out-turn meeting – progress against objectives, savings and reinvestment, and management value for money.

Agreement between all parties is needed where our contracting intentions significantly impact on authority purchasing. The annual review provides an opportunity to explore key performance issues on each side to improve the effectiveness of overall purchasing for the population.

Over/underspends and risk

The commission holds no reserve to deal with our overspending, so monitoring must be early and decisive. Budgets based on historical activity, boundary changes (Bath has moved from Wiltshire to Avon) and a relatively small risk pool of 60 000 population necessitates a tight risk strategy. Calculations show remarkably little variation between the four practices in terms of low-cost, high-volume episodes, and most high-cost, low-volume care is in any case blocked back. However, to be on the safe side we have agreed that 1% of 'live' contract funds, to be managed by the authority, will be paid to the authority as an insurance premium against excess activity.

We are limited to 5% savings, these on 'live' contracts only, to be planned in advance and reinvested by agreement with the authority. Unplanned savings will be returned. These arrangements appear to be more stringent than in many other such pilots, but we are within a resource losing district that is also supporting an overspent acute Trust.

The four practices

Each of the four practices has taken the lead on a specific area, as outlined below.

Practice 1 – Information

Much work has been done validating activity provided by the commission and the local Trusts. Our staff have checked through lists of FCEs, checking practice against provider against authority, quite crucial as the baseline for budgets is historical activity and if we get it wrong now ...! Despite the authority staff having worked hard on producing activity data, our main concern remains their accuracy.

Most of the local Trusts have been very quick to respond to and co-operate in providing the required information, which we feel certain has been facilitated by their early inclusion in our meetings and discussions. One of our pitfalls has been that they were not included early enough.

During the first four years of fundholding at our own practice, we had been recording most of the non-fundholding activity on our own networked system. This helped with the validation of provider and commission data. Together with our existing fundholder computer software supplier, we designed a total purchasing package to run along-side fundholding. This was fully operational from April 1995, recording all total purchasing activity where it was available. This has been particularly interesting with A&E, as we have been recording:

- method of arrival at the A&E department, for example GP, self-referral or road traffic accident

- presenting problem – for example abdominal pain, poisoning or chest pain

- final diagnosis using ICD10 codes

- outcome – home, admitted, died, etc.

The same process has applied to emergency admissions, and it is hoped that this information will assist the debate that will have to take place at national level if we are to control the rise in emergency admissions, or purchase episodes of care and not multiple FCEs.

In conjunction with the local maternity unit, we designed a manual tracking form that would follow the patient through the system from antenatal booking through to postnatal discharge, recording every event. The unit is designing a computer program incorporating the manual format into their new software.

Practice 2 – Long-term mental health services

Total purchasing involves taking on inpatient work, including high-cost, low-volume cases such as those with anorexia nervosa and high-security patients. Although the mental health Trust has been able to give us 'snapshot' data, these were not robust enough to purchase other than by block contract in the first year, 1995/6. In response the Trust is providing increasingly accurate data that will be matched to HRGs when they become available for psychiatry, producing care plans for long-stay patients and involving GPs in discussions on individual tertiary referrals. More and more people are being transferred from prison facilities into the NHS, but finance does not follow the patient from the Home Office to the Health Service. These long-term, high-cost patients are unpredictable and make a mockery of any budgetary planning at practice level. One of the practices in the pilot faces just this challenge, with the cost of one case alone being equivalent to its total hospital ECR budget (£165 000 *per annum*). Committal of such large sums, at short notice and potentially for decades, reinforces the need for a centrally based risk insurance policy. The practices are co-operating with the authority and the Trust to provide a local intensive care facility to reduce the number of patients cared for in the regional secure unit, thus benefiting patients and families as well as making a likely cost saving. Another area under scrutiny is the complex interaction between social services and psychiatry especially prevalent in the elderly population.

Practice 3 – Community hospitals and emergency admissions

To get to grips with rising emergency admissions and the increasing pressure on acute hospital beds, together with underutilization of community beds and delayed discharges generally, the two Trowbridge practices jointly employed a primary care liaison manager (PCLM). Her brief is to manage the interface between primary and secondary care, and her appointment has been a huge success. One of the Adcroft's (one of the four practices) objectives was to gain an understanding of acute admissions, the source, the reason, the length of stay and place of discharge, and to develop an understanding of the consequences of admission and outcome, for example moving to tertiary centres, a waiting list or community beds.

The PCLM is in daily contact with all admissions to ensure that they are appropriate and in the appropriate place. An experienced nurse practitioner, she is helping us to understand the reasons for unduly long admissions and has promoted the concept of discharge planning on admission to make sure that patients are socially organized as well as medically fit for discharge. Her role has been widely accepted and welcomed by both the acute and community Trusts. She is currently paid from the management allowance, but it is hoped that the reductions in bed occupation that she will bring about may well be sufficient to assure her permanent future.

Practice 4 – Maternity and social services

Historically the Bath district is fortunate to have a community based maternity service where 40% of all deliveries take place either in one of seven isolated GP units (of which Trowbridge and Frome are two) or at home. Wiltshire Health Centre, the community Trust, hires back the acute unit in Bath from the acute Trust and has the director of maternity services as its medical director. It is broadly accepted, certainly by midwives, that uncomplicated pregnancies should be delivered as near home as possible, even for the primiparous. Except for key personnel, the midwives are already fully integrated between the community and the community and acute units. They are attached to practices in the same way as are community nursing staff and have admitting rights. Mothers have been carrying their own notes for many years.

Consequently the local service is further ahead than most in matching up to the ten points of the Changing Childbirth initiative within a flexible framework. With seven isolated GP units, the GP obstetric input is also higher than average, but modern pressures of litigation and a diminishing skill base are putting younger GPs off continuing in this role.

To progress further towards the aims of Changing Childbirth, we are examining the possibilities of autonomous team midwifery. Teams will need to be of sufficient size to cover each other for nights spent working, holidays and sickness with a realistic case load, for example seven midwives to 300 deliveries *per annum*, thus covering a population of approximately 30 000. The moving midwife, travelling into hospital with the mother-to-be, should reduce the number of permanent hospital staff required and entirely take over the community function. With willing obstetric help, the aim is to train midwives to suture, read cardiographs properly, put up drips, augment labour, use a ventouse, resuscitate flat babies and accept responsibility for being the lead carer. The challenge for our GPs is to let go of control and paternalism while at the same time providing the support the midwives need in their new enhanced role and the continuity of the long-term source of knowledge that family doctors have and wish to exercise.

To be equitable and manageable, such changes need to be introduced district-wide and involve all practices, some of which are non-fund-holding. Contracting independently for an individual team is as yet unrealistic, although it will start as a shadow to examine difficulties such as grading of staff and their accountability.

As a result of the information from the maternity tracking forms, we aim to reduce the number of attendances while making them more focused on what mothers and families tell us they want, and to change the currency of purchasing from FCEs to HRGs.

AVON **Bath** Oldfield Park 10 500 patients District general hospital	WILTSHIRE **Trowbridge** Adcroft 8500 patients Lovemead 14 000 patients Community hospital

SOMERSET
Frome
Frome medical practice
26 000 patients
Community hospital

Total pilot population: 59 000 representing 7.5% of the Wilts and Bath Health Authority.

District general hospital: Royal United Hospital, Bath; 400-bed comprehensive secondary care centre.

Community hospitals: each have 30–40 GP and geriatric beds, comprehensive outpatients department, X-ray, physiotherapy, 24-hour nurse staffed, GP-supervised minor injuries units and a maternity department.

Figure 12.1: The geography of the pilot.

Social services

The health authority and Wiltshire Social Services have promoted link workers, housed and active within the practices as part of the primary care team and, from 1996, practice-attached mainstream social workers. The continuing care element of the social services budget is being broken down to practice level, to be shared along with the practice's element of the community care budget in joint commissioning.

Conclusion

The attitude of partners not directly involved in total purchasing and of commission staff fearful of the consequences, together with the accusation of putting money before patient care and the feeling that one is not really doing anything worthwhile, can lead to moments of despair, but if we are to have a primary care-led NHS, control our work-load and give our patients the individual service that we, as patients, would expect, total purchasing with all its vicissitudes must win through.

If there is one message to leave it is to get all the interested parties involved from the earliest outset.

Checklist for total purchasing preparatory year

Organizational

- Project board – who should be on it, what its terms of reference are, and how often should it meet.

- Purchasing forum – how purchasing decisions are made, who makes them, etc.

- Project management, central co-ordination – recommend project manager, who project manager reports to, where he or she sits, what the role is.

- Relationships between GPs and the authority – need to forge close links with all departments, needs strong financial and public health involvement in particular, at director level.

- Need 'agreement' between health authority and GPs to ensure that both sides are clear about accountability, limits of responsibility, basis on which the project is operating, what happens about overspends, underspends, etc.

Budget setting

- Need to agree mechanism.

- Carry out as early as possible.

- Monitor shadow contracts against shadow budget.

- Agree what to do about any gap (either way) between historic and capitation budgets.

Purchasing

- Is any needs assessment to be carried out? What is public health input to purchasing?
- Develop purchasing plan.
- Look at risk management – how to deal with high-cost, low-incidence areas, for example psychiatry, bone marrow transplants, ECRs in general.
- Use of information to inform purchasing decisions and service developments/changes.

Contracting

- Provider prices need to be sensitive, particularly to length of stay – start talking to providers early on.
- Which providers will you contract with directly and which via the health authority?
- Start service development discussions early, for example with A&E, general medicine, community providers, etc.
- How will you carry out contract negotiations?

Procedures

- General contract management procedures – what is done by practices, what is done by the commission.
- ECRs – administration and authorization.
- Invoices and internal budget transfer procedures for services bought via the health authority.
- Monitoring direct contracts.
- Monitoring external contracts.

Develop protocols

- A&E.
- Use of nurses in patients' homes.
- Use of community hospitals.
- Emergency admissions, etc.

Evaluation

- Internal – liaison with public health and purchasing to carry out research studies, service reviews, etc. and inform on effectiveness.
- External – is there going to be any external evaluation?

Communication

- Press.
- Patients.
- CHC.

Information

- Document information requirements – these to some extent depend on priority areas for service developments.
- Discuss with providers your information requirements – particularly with community Trusts as they may not be able to supply patient specific data at first.
- Validate data in practices.
- Use for shadow monitoring – but costing is a lot of work.

System

- Decide configuration (based on who will do what).
- Procure.
- Install.

Appendix 2

Terms of reference for purchasing forum

BIPP purchasing forum

The purchasing forum consists of one GP from each of the participating practices, four health authority representatives (one from each of the information, finance, public health and purchasing directorates), the project manager and the BIPP purchasing manager. There is no provider representation on the purchasing forum, although there may be provider involvement in sub-groups set up by the forum.

Overall remit

To be responsible for the purchasing and contract monitoring aspects of the project, including remaining within budget. In particular:

* to develop a BIPP purchasing strategy, relating this to policies and strategies of fundholders, health authority and FHSA, and if necessary agree divergence from these strategies

* to identify potential changes in services for 1996/7 and to oversee discussions with providers regarding these changes

* to make purchasing decisions aligned with the defined purchasing strategy and to negotiate contracts (or oversee the negotiations)

* to oversee sub-groups and purchasing teams tasked to work on particular areas

* to agree a method for calculating the purchasing allocation for BIPP and to agree the calculations once health authority and fundholding allocations are known

* to agree monitoring mechanisms for contracts

* to monitor contracts

* to agree procedures for ECR authorization and monitoring

- to monitor ECR activity and expenditure against budget
- to agree protocols for referrals
- to consider the effects of BIPP contracts on non-BIPP patients.

Accountability

The purchasing forum is a sub-committee of the health authority and is accountable to the health authority board for the use of the BIPP purchasing allocation.

Appendix 3

Structure of project initiation document

Project initiation document

Author:

Date:

Version no.:

1 Introduction

    1.1 About this document
    1.2 Background to the project
    1.3 Other similar projects

2 Terms of reference

    2.1 Purpose and objectives
    2.2 Scope
    2.3 Constraints
    2.4 Assumptions

3 Organization structure

    3.1 Introduction
    3.2 Project management structure
    3.3 Purchasing structure
    3.4 Diagrammatic representation

4 Plan description

    4.1 Overview of approach
    4.2 Milestones
    4.3 Resources

Relevant executive letters and other guidance

The following executive letters may be of use to total purchasing pilots.

| EL(95)54 | An Accountability Framework for GP Fundholding |
| EL(94)79 | Developing NHS Purchasing and GP Fundholding |

Purchasing – general

EL(95)68	Priorities and Planning Guidance for the NHS 1996/97
EL(93)98	Contracting for Specialised Services
EL(95)97	New Drugs for Multiple Sclerosis

Mental health

| HSG(94)27 | Guidance on the Discharge of Mentally Disordered People and their Care in the Community |
| EL(92)6 | Services for Mentally Disordered Offenders and Patients with Similar Needs |

Effectiveness

EL(93)115	Improving Clinical Effectiveness
EL(94)74	Improving Clinical Effectiveness
EL(95)105	Improving the Effectiveness of Clinical Services
EL(95)13	Effectiveness – a Vision for the Future
EL(94)20	Clinical Audit 94/95 and Beyond

Maternity

| EL(94)9 | Woman-centred Maternity Services |
| EL(94)41 | The Patient's Charter and Maternity Services |

Continuing care

| HSG(95)8/LAC(95)5 | NHS Responsibilities for Meeting Continuing Care Needs |
| EL(95)39 | Community Care Monitoring |

ECRs
HSG(95)8   Guidance on Operation and Notification Arrange-
                     ments for Tertiary Extra-contractual Referrals
HSG(95)20   Guidance on the Revised Operation of Notification
                     Arrangements for Tertiary Extra-contractual
                     Referrals

A list of further reading is available in the appendices of the document
'Priorities and Planning Guidance for the NHS 1996/97'.

Spend profile

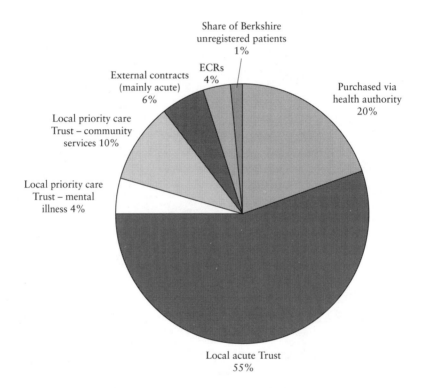

Index